The B♭ Real Dixieland Book

Arrangements by Robert Rawlins

ISBN 978-1-4803-5527-9

7777 W. BLUEMOUND RD. P.O. BOX 13819 MILWAUKEE, WI 53213

For all works contained herein:
Unauthorized copying, arranging, adapting, recording, Internet posting, public performance,
or other distribution of the printed music in this publication is an infringement of copyright.
Infringers are liable under the law.

Visit Hal Leonard Online at
www.halleonard.com

Eddie Condon once introduced his pianist by telling about their first job together. "He was showing me some new chords on 'China Boy' and I asked him his name—his name turned out to be Jess Stacy." Condon continued with, "Jess is going to show us some new chords for 'Sweet Lorraine' this afternoon."

New chords? Yes, that's what jazz musicians have always done, from Buddy Bolden to Louis Armstrong to Wynton Marsalis, and everyone in between, regardless of style. They not only improvise new solos every time they play a tune—they work out their own arrangements with their own interpretation of the harmony, melody, and just about every other musical element.

So what's in this book, the original version of each song? Not exactly. It's not that simple. A great number of tunes that became Dixieland classics were not written for jazz bands at all, and musicians took liberties with both melody and harmony (let alone rhythm!) from the start.

Even when established jazz musicians wrote original material, the published sheet music often differed substantially from the way the song was actually recorded. Sheet music was intended for purchase by the general public, most likely for amateur performance on the parlor piano. Therefore, the original sheet music may involve harmonic progressions that are not suited to jazz performance. Listening to solo piano recordings of Hoagy Carmichael and Fats Waller, for example, confirms that they took great liberties with their own music.

So what are the sources for this book? For starters, the original sheet music was consulted for most songs. Wherever possible and practical, both verse and lyrics are included. But the underlying premise of this collection is that guidance was to be found in the definitive recordings, not the publications. Jazz evolved out of an aural tradition—an exchange of ideas on the streets and in the nightclubs. It stands to reason that the way the songs should be performed will be found by listening to the musicians themselves, not consulting a written score.

The chords, melodies, and arrangements provided in this book result from talking to hundreds of musicians and listening to countless recordings. As you can imagine, there is never total agreement on the best way to play a tune, which is exactly how it should be. Jazz is a vibrant, dynamic, constantly changing music. What I have attempted to do is provide lead sheets that offer maximum flexibility while providing information that reflects the way tunes are commonly played.

For the most part, I've attempted to include only essential chords. Musicians are free to add their favorite turnarounds, lead-in chords, and passing chords during static harmonic areas. My intention was to keep the page uncluttered. While adding such chords is certainly characteristic of the style and can add harmonic interest, I didn't want to box in the performer with my prescriptions. Listening to historic recordings reveals that these "in between" chords are rarely essential to the tune, and when added would sometimes vary from chorus to chorus.

In keeping with historic practice, the majority of chords are triads and dominant 7ths. Dixieland, like other forms of jazz, is a very flexible music, and extended chords will certainly work in many circumstances. But, again, my goal was to provide information, not a prescription. Musicians can work from the basic information provided and make their own choices. One exception is diminished chords, which are indicated as diminished 7ths. Recorded solos make it clear that horn players heard diminished chords as four-note structures, even when the rhythm section was playing triads.

Many Dixieland tunes are multi-part extended pieces, resembling marches or rags. (In fact, several of the tunes in this book ARE marches and rags!) The recorded evidence reveals that there is no single correct way to navigate through such tunes, and it is by no means necessary to play every section. Musicians viewed the form of these pieces loosely, and seemed to consider it their duty to rearrange and reinvent existing versions. It is certainly not the intention of this book to choose one historic performance and reassemble that arrangement. I just wanted to provide the material, in an accurate and usable format, so that bands could adapt the music to their own purposes.

A wide variety of Dixieland and traditional jazz tunes have been included in this book, covering just about every possible era, style, and interpretation of the music. For various reasons, some involving access, copyright permission, and space issues, every desirable tune could not be included, and even a few of the classics are missing from this book. But every inclusion was carefully chosen and fully researched. Musicians will find abundant material for performing traditional jazz, and even seasoned veterans of the style will surely come across some lyric, verse, or tune that proves to be a valuable addition to their repertoire.

Robert Rawlins

A

ACE IN THE HOLE	10
AFTER I SAY I'M SORRY	9
AFTER YOU'VE GONE	12
AIN'T MISBEHAVIN'	14
AIN'T SHE SWEET	16
ALABAMA JUBILEE	18
ALABAMY BOUND	20
THE ALCOHOLIC BLUES	22
ALEXANDER'S RAGTIME BAND	24
ALICE BLUE GOWN	26
ALL BY MYSELF	28
ANGRY	30
AS LONG AS I LIVE	27
AT A GEORGIA CAMP MEETING	32
AT SUNDOWN	33
AUNT HAGAR'S BLUES	34
AVALON	36

B

BABY FACE	38
BABY, WON'T YOU PLEASE COME HOME	37
BACK IN YOUR OWN BACKYARD	40
BALLIN' THE JACK	42
BASIN STREET BLUES	44
BEALE STREET BLUES	46
BEI MIR BIST DU SCHÖN (MEANS THAT YOU'RE GRAND)	48
BETWEEN THE DEVIL AND THE DEEP BLUE SEA	45
BILL BAILEY, WON'T YOU PLEASE COME HOME	50
THE BIRTH OF THE BLUES	52
(WHAT DID I DO TO BE SO) BLACK AND BLUE	54
BLACK BOTTOM STOMP	56
BLUE AND BROKEN HEARTED	55
THE BLUE ROOM	58
BLUE SKIES	60
BLUE TURNING GREY OVER YOU	62
BLUES MY NAUGHTY SWEETIE GAVE TO ME	64
BLUIN' THE BLUES	66
BORNEO	61
BREEZIN' ALONG WITH THE BREEZE	68
BUGLE CALL RAG	70
BY AND BY	71
BYE BYE BLUES	72

C

CAKE WALKING BABIES FROM HOME	74
CALIFORNIA, HERE I COME	73
CANAL STREET BLUES	76
CARELESS LOVE	77
CHICAGO (THAT TODDLIN' TOWN)	78
CHICAGO BREAKDOWN (STRATFORD HUNCH)	80
CHIMES BLUES	82
CHINA BOY	81
CHINATOWN, MY CHINATOWN	84
CLARINET MARMALADE	86
COME BACK SWEET PAPA	88
COPENHAGEN	90
CORNET CHOP SUEY	92
A COTTAGE FOR SALE	85
CRAZY RHYTHM	94
THE CURSE OF AN ACHING HEART	95

D

DANGEROUS BLUES	96
DARDANELLA	98

D (cont.)

THE DARKTOWN STRUTTERS' BALL 100
DEAR OLD SOUTHLAND...................... 102
'DEED I DO 103
DIG-A-DIG-A-DOO 104
DILL PICKLES 105
DINAH 106
DIPPERMOUTH BLUES...................... 108
DO YOU KNOW WHAT IT MEANS TO MISS
    NEW ORLEANS 110
DOCTOR JAZZ 112
DON'T GET AROUND MUCH ANYMORE... 114
DOWN BY THE RIVERSIDE 116
DOWN HOME RAG 117
DOWN IN JUNGLE TOWN 118

E

EAST ST. LOUIS TOODLE-OO 120
EVERYBODY LOVES MY BABY
    (BUT MY BABY DON'T LOVE
    NOBODY BUT ME)..................... 122
EXACTLY LIKE YOU 124

F

FAREWELL BLUES.............................. 125
THE FISH MAN (LE MARCHAND
    DE POISSONS)....................... 126
FIVE FOOT TWO, EYES OF BLUE (HAS
    ANYBODY SEEN MY GIRL?)........ 127
FLOATIN' DOWN TO COTTON TOWN........ 128

G

GEE BABY, AIN'T I GOOD TO YOU 130
GEORGIA ON MY MIND 131
A GOOD MAN IS HARD TO FIND............ 132
GOODBYE....................................... 134
GRANDPA'S SPELLS............................ 135
GRIZZLY BEAR................................. 136

H

HARD HEARTED HANNAH
    (THE VAMP OF SAVANNAH) 140
HEEBIE JEEBIES................................ 138
HIGH SOCIETY 142
HINDUSTAN 144
HOME (WHEN SHADOWS FALL)............ 139
HONEYSUCKLE ROSE.......................... 148
HOTTER THAN THAT.......................... 146
A HUNDRED YEARS FROM TODAY........ 150

I

I AIN'T GONNA GIVE NOBODY NONE O' THIS
    JELLY ROLL 147
I CAN'T BELIEVE THAT YOU'RE IN
    LOVE WITH ME...................... 152
I CAN'T GIVE YOU ANYTHING
    BUT LOVE................................ 153
I GOTTA RIGHT TO SING THE BLUES 154
I NEVER KNEW 155
I NEVER KNEW (I COULD LOVE ANYBODY
    LIKE I'M LOVING YOU) 156
I WANT A BIG BUTTER AND EGG MAN.. 157
I WISH I COULD SHIMMY LIKE MY
    SISTER KATE......................... 160
I'M CONFESSIN' (THAT I LOVE YOU) 158
I'M CRAZY 'BOUT MY BABY (AND MY
    BABY'S CRAZY 'BOUT ME) 162
I'M GONNA SIT RIGHT DOWN AND WRITE
    MYSELF A LETTER.................... 159
I'M GONNA STOMP MR. HENRY LEE...... 164
I'VE FOUND A NEW BABY
    (I FOUND A NEW BABY)............. 166
I'VE GOT A FEELING I'M FALLING......... 168
IDA, SWEET AS APPLE CIDER 165
IN A SHANTY IN OLD SHANTY TOWN.... 170
INDIANA (BACK HOME AGAIN
    IN INDIANA)......................... 172
IRISH BLACK BOTTOM 174
IS IT TRUE WHAT THEY SAY
    ABOUT DIXIE........................... 176

I (cont.)

IT ALL DEPENDS ON YOU...................... 178
IT DON'T MEAN A THING
       (IF IT AIN'T GOT THAT SWING).. 179

J

JA-DA 180
THE JAPANESE SANDMAN 182
THE JAZZ-ME BLUES........................... 184
JELLY ROLL BLUES............................. 186
JITTERBUG WALTZ.............................. 188
JOHNSON RAG 189
JUBILEE 190
JUNE NIGHT 191
JUST A CLOSER WALK WITH THEE 192

K

KANSAS CITY STOMP........................... 194
KEEPIN' OUT OF MISCHIEF NOW 193
KING PORTER STOMP.......................... 196

L

LAZY RIVER 198
LAZYBONES 200
LIFE IS JUST A BOWL OF CHERRIES 202
LIMEHOUSE BLUES 204
LINGER AWHILE................................. 199
LIVERY STABLE BLUES
      (BARNYARD BLUES)................... 206
THE LONESOME ROAD......................... 207
LOUISIANA....................................... 208
LOVE IS JUST AROUND THE CORNER 210
THE LOVE NEST 211

M

MAHOGANY HALL STOMP..................... 212
MAKIN' WHOOPEE! 214

MANDY.. 216
MANDY MAKE UP YOUR MIND............. 218
MAPLE LEAF RAG............................... 220
MARGIE 217
MEAN TO ME 222
MEMORIES OF YOU 223
MEMPHIS BLUES................................ 224
MIDNIGHT IN MOSCOW........................ 226
THE MINOR DRAG
      (THE DRAGSTER DRAG) 227
MISSISSIPPI MUD 228
MUSKRAT RAMBLE.............................. 230
MY BABY JUST CARES FOR ME............ 232
MY BLUE HEAVEN 234
MY BUDDY.. 235
MY GAL SAL...................................... 236
MY HONEY'S LOVING ARMS.................. 238
MY MELANCHOLY BABY 240
MY MONDAY DATE.............................. 237

N

NAGASAKI 242
NEW ORLEANS 244
NOBODY KNOWS YOU WHEN YOU'RE
      DOWN AND OUT........................ 245
NOBODY'S SWEETHEART...................... 246

O

OH BY JINGO! OH BY GEE! YOU'RE
      THE ONLY GIRL FOR ME 248
OH! DIDN'T HE RAMBLE 249
ON THE ALAMO 250
ORIENTAL STRUT 252
ORIGINAL DIXIELAND ONE-STEP 254
ORY'S CREOLE TROMBONE................... 256

P

PADDLIN' MADELIN' HOME................... 258
PALESTEENA 260

P (cont.)

PANAMA 262
THE PEARLS 264
PEG O' MY HEART 259
PETITE FLEUR (LITTLE FLOWER) 266
PLEASE 268
POOR BUTTERFLY 270
POTATO HEAD BLUES 272
PRETTY BABY 274
P.S. I LOVE YOU 269
PUTTIN' ON THE RITZ 276

R

RED SAILS IN THE SUNSET 278
RIVERBOAT SHUFFLE 280
ROCKIN' CHAIR 282
ROSE OF WASHINGTON SQUARE 284
ROSE ROOM 286
ROSES OF PICARDY 288
ROSETTA 289
ROYAL GARDEN BLUES 290
RUNNIN' WILD 292

S

SAILING DOWN THE
      CHESAPEAKE BAY 294
SAINT JAMES INFIRMARY 291
ST. LOUIS BLUES 296
SAN 298
SHAKE THAT THING 299
SHE'S FUNNY THAT WAY 300
THE SHEIK OF ARABY 302
SHINE 301
SHREVEPORT STOMPS 304
SIDEWALK BLUES 306
SINGIN' THE BLUES TILL MY DADDY
      COMES HOME 308
SMILE 309
SMILES 310

SOME OF THESE DAYS 311
SOMEBODY LOVES ME 312
SOMEBODY STOLE MY GAL 313
SOMEDAY YOU'LL BE SORRY 314
SOUTH 315
S'POSIN' 316
SQUEEZE ME 318
STEALIN' APPLES 319
STOMPIN' AT THE SAVOY 320
STRUT MISS LIZZIE 321
STRUTTIN' WITH SOME BARBECUE 322
SWEET SUE-JUST YOU 323
SWING THAT MUSIC 324

T

'TAIN'T NOBODY'S BIZ-NESS IF I DO 325
THAT DA-DA STRAIN 326
THAT'S A PLENTY 327
THERE'LL BE SOME CHANGES MADE 330
THERE'LL COME A TIME WHEN YOU'LL
      NEED ME 332
THOU SWELL 333
THREE LITTLE WORDS 334
TIGER RAG (HOLD THAT TIGER) 336
TIN ROOF BLUES 335
TISHOMINGO BLUES 338
TUCK ME TO SLEEP IN MY OLD
      TUCKY HOME 340
TWELFTH STREET RAG 341
TWELFTH STREET RAG
      (DIXIELAND VERSION) 342

U

UNDECIDED 344

W

WABASH BLUES 346
WALKIN' MY BABY BACK HOME 348

W (cont.)

THE WANG WANG BLUES 350
WASHINGTON AND LEE SWING 343
'WAY DOWN YONDER IN
    NEW ORLEANS 352
WEARY BLUES 353
WEST END BLUES 354
WHEN IT'S SLEEPY TIME
    DOWN SOUTH 356
WHEN MY BABY SMILES AT ME 355
WHEN MY SUGAR WALKS DOWN
    THE STREET 358
WHEN THE SAINTS GO MARCHING IN ... 360
WHEN YOU'RE SMILING (THE WHOLE
    WORLD SMILES WITH YOU) 361
WHERE DID ROBINSON CRUSOE GO WITH
    FRIDAY ON SATURDAY NIGHT? ... 362

WHISPERING 364
WILD CHERRIES 366
WOLVERINE BLUES 368
THE WORLD IS WAITING FOR
    THE SUNRISE 370
WRAP YOUR TROUBLES IN DREAMS
    (AND DREAM YOUR
    TROUBLES AWAY) 372

Y

YELLOW DOG BLUES 374
YOU ALWAYS HURT THE ONE
    YOU LOVE 371
YOU CAN DEPEND ON ME 376
YOU TOOK ADVANTAGE OF ME 377
YOU'RE THE CREAM IN MY COFFEE 378

ACE IN THE HOLE

— JAMES DEMPSEY/GEORGE MITCHELL

(RUBATO)

VERSE

1. This town is full of guys, Who think they're might-y wise,
2. The more you go a-round, in good old Nash-ville town, You'll

Just be-cause they know a thing or two. You'll see them night and day, Strol-ling
find that what I say to you is true. They'll meet you with a smile, but

up and down Broad-way, Tell-ing of the won-ders they can do. There's
you know all the while, That they're try-ing to spring some-thing new. The

con men and there's boost-ers, There's card sharks and crap shoot-ers, They
things they're al-ways tell-ing, of the lem-ons that they're sell-ing, And the

con-gre-gate a-round the Met-ro-pole. They wear
hun-dreds that they spend in buy-ing clothes. Ev-'ry

flash-y ties and col-lars, But where they get their dol-lars,
one knows they're re-ly-ing, it's the ace-s do the buy-ing, That

CHORUS (MED. SWING)

They all have an ace down in the hole. Some of them write_
dress them from their heads down to their toes. Some of them write_

to the old folks for dough,_
to the old folks for coin,_

Copyright © 2010 by HAL LEONARD CORPORATION

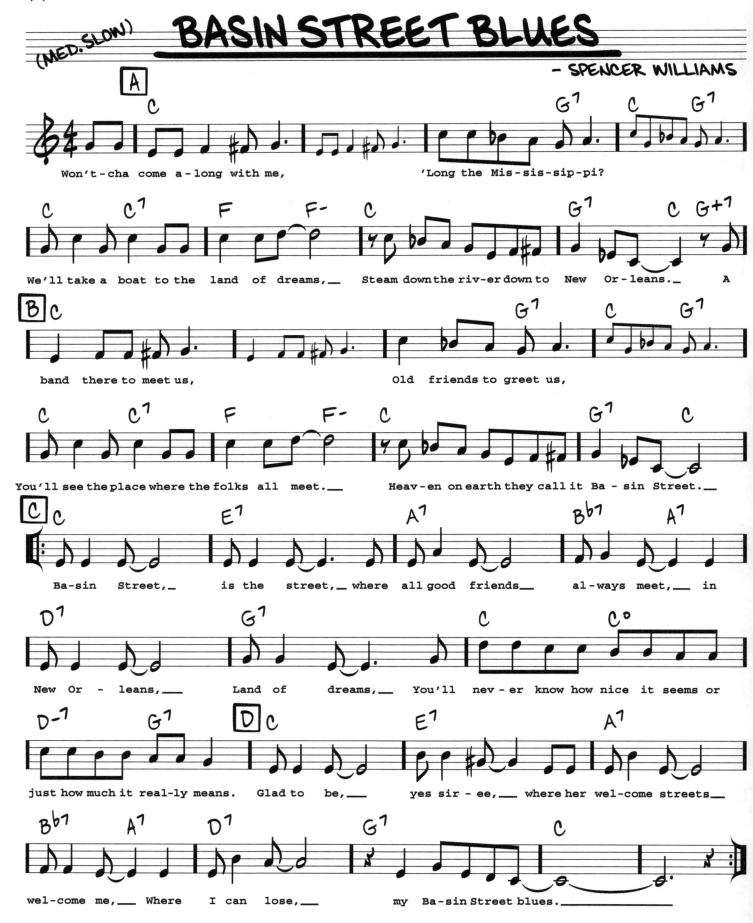

(WHAT DID I DO TO BE SO) BLACK AND BLUE

MED. BALLAD

- ANDY RAZAF/HARRY BROOKS/FATS WALLER

1. Cold emp-ty bed, springs hard as lead, pains in my head,
2. Just 'cause you're black, folks think you lack. They laugh at you,

feel like Old Ned, What did I do to be so black and blue?
and scorn you too, What did I do to be so black and blue?

No joys for me, no com-pan-y; e-ven the mouse ran from my house,
When you are near, they laugh and sneer; set you a-side, and you're de-nied,

All my life through, I've been so black and blue.
what did I do to be so black and blue?

I'm white in-side, it don't help my case.
How sad I am, each day I feel worse.

'Cause I can't hide what is on my face, ooh!
My mark of Ham seems to be a curse, ooh!

I'm so for-lorn, life's just a thorn, my heart is torn, why was I born?
How will it end? Ain't got a friend, my on-ly sin is in my skin.

What did I do to be so black and blue?
What did I do to be so black and blue?

Copyright © 1929 by Chappell & Co., EMI Mills Music Inc. and Razaf Music in the United States
Copyright Renewed

Dogfight

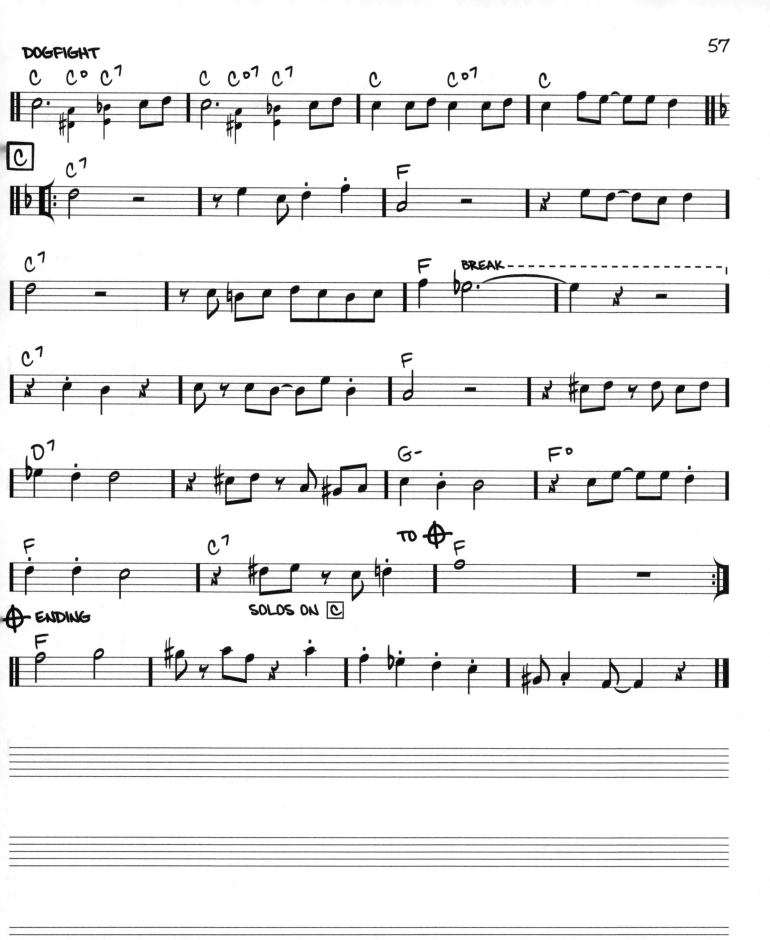

3rd Chorus:

Blues that you get from Sweetie, when she phones to another guy.
And there are blues when your honey spends all of your money,
And blues when she tells you a lie.
There are blues that you get when married, wishing that you could be free.
But the kind of blues that's good and blue come from buying wine for two:
The kind of blues my sweetie give to me.

Patter Chorus (stop time):

There are blues you get from women when you see 'em goin' swimmin',
and you haven't got a bathin' suit yourself.
There are blues that get you quicker when you've had a lot of liquor,
And someone goes and takes it off the shelf!

There are blues you get from waitin' on the dock,
Wondrin' if the boat's gonna rock.
There are blues you get from gettin' in a taxi cab and frettin'
Each time you hear the bumper jump the clock.

There are blues you get from tryin' to keep your Uncle Bill from dyin',
And he afterward forgets you in his will.
There are blues you get from kisses when you're walkin' with the missus,
And a chorus girl shouts, "Hi, Bill!"

There are blues that make you quiver gonna make you shake and shiver,
But the blues that make you want to end it all in the river,
Are the blues my naughty sweetie gives to me!

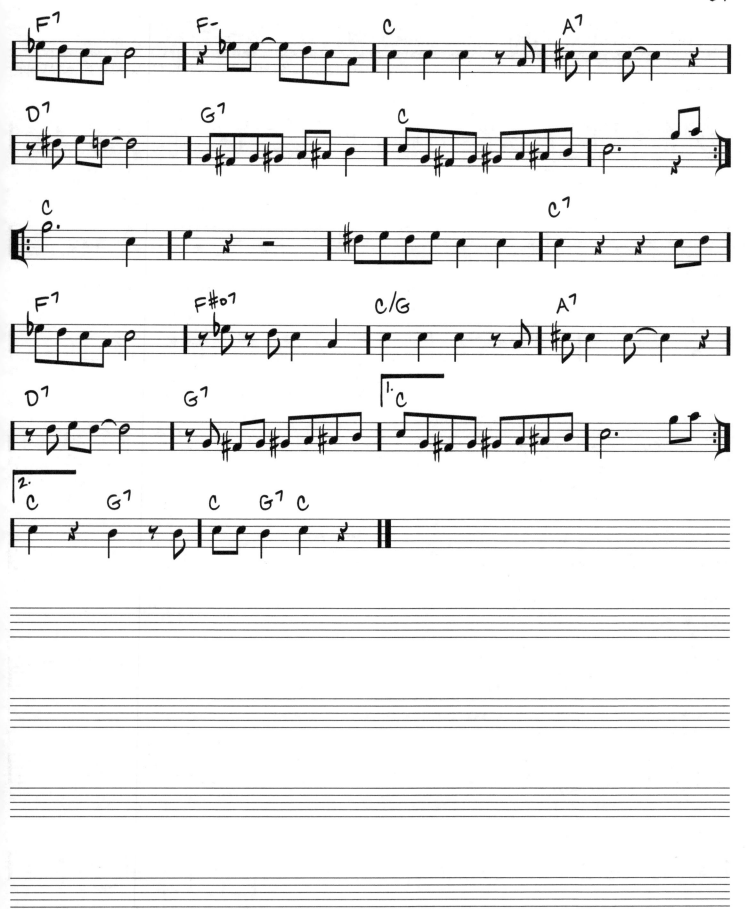

Additional verses:
We are often destitute
of the things that life demands,
want of food and want of shelter,
thirsty hills and barren lands;
we are trusting in the Lord,
and according to God's Word,
we will understand it better by and by.

Temptations, hidden snares
often take us unawares,
and our hearts are made to bleed
for a thoughtless word or deed;
and we wonder why the test
when we try to do our best,
but we'll understand it better by and by.

Copyright © 2010 by HAL LEONARD CORPORATION

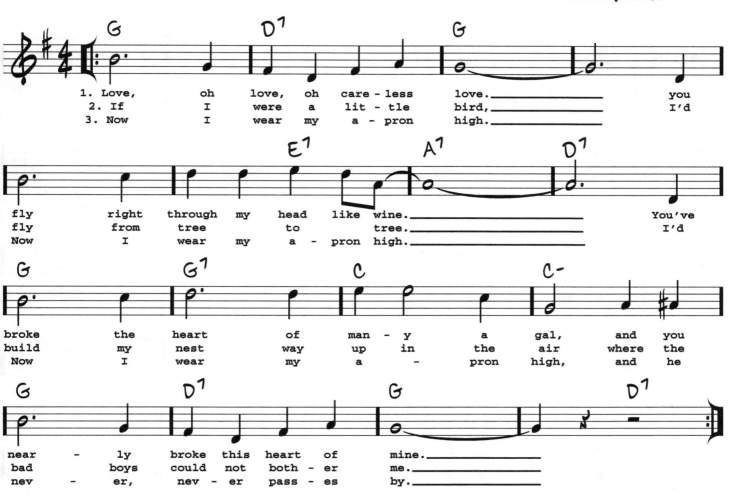

Love, oh love, oh careless love,
You fly to the head like wine
You've wrecked the life of many a poor gal
And you nearly spoiled this life of mine.

Love, oh love, oh careless love,
In your clutches of desire
You've made me break a many true vow
Then you set my very soul on fire.

Love, oh love, oh careless love,
All my happiness bereft
You've filled my heart with weary old blues
Now I'm walkin' talkin' to myself.

Love, oh love, oh careless love,
Trusted you now its too late
You've made me throw my only friend down
That is why I sing this hymn of hate.

Love, oh love, oh careless love,
Night and day I weep and moan
You brought the wrong man into my life
For my sins till judgement I'll atone.

Love, oh love, oh careless love,
Here is all that I can say
Just like a Gypsy I'm roamin' 'round
And just can't keep the blues away.

Love, oh love, oh careless love,
Like a thief comes in the night
You came into this glad heart of mine
Then you put my happiness to flight.

Copyright © 2010 by HAL LEONARD CORPORATION

CHICAGO (THAT TODDLIN' TOWN)

(RUBATO)

– FRED FISHER

VERSE

1. I got a gal, I got a pal, I got a chance, I got a dance, wait-ing for me. _____
2. An-y old maid who's not a-fraid, pow-ders her nose, puts on nice clothes, she get a beau. _____

I'm goin' to make, right to the lake. There with the boys, in Ill-in-ois, I want to be. _____
An-y old guy o-ver in Chi, he's got a chance, if he can dance, he'll cop a Flo. _____

You may not care for to be there, but I de-clare you're not a-ware just where to go. _____
tel that's a bit swell must have a band right here on hand, or else they're cheap. _____

When you're in town, just call a-round, right there I'm found. Real-ly you ought to know: _____
If you'll in-vest, you'll find a guest, they'll nev-er rest, they're danc-ing while they sleep: _____

CHORUS

Chi - ca - go, ___ Chi - ca - go, ___ that tod-dl'-ing town, ___ tod-dl'-ing town. ___ Chi - ca - go, ___ Chi - ca - go, ___ I'll show you a-round, ___ I love it. Bet your bot-tom dol-lar you'll lose the blues_ in Chi-

Copyright © 2010 by HAL LEONARD CORPORATION

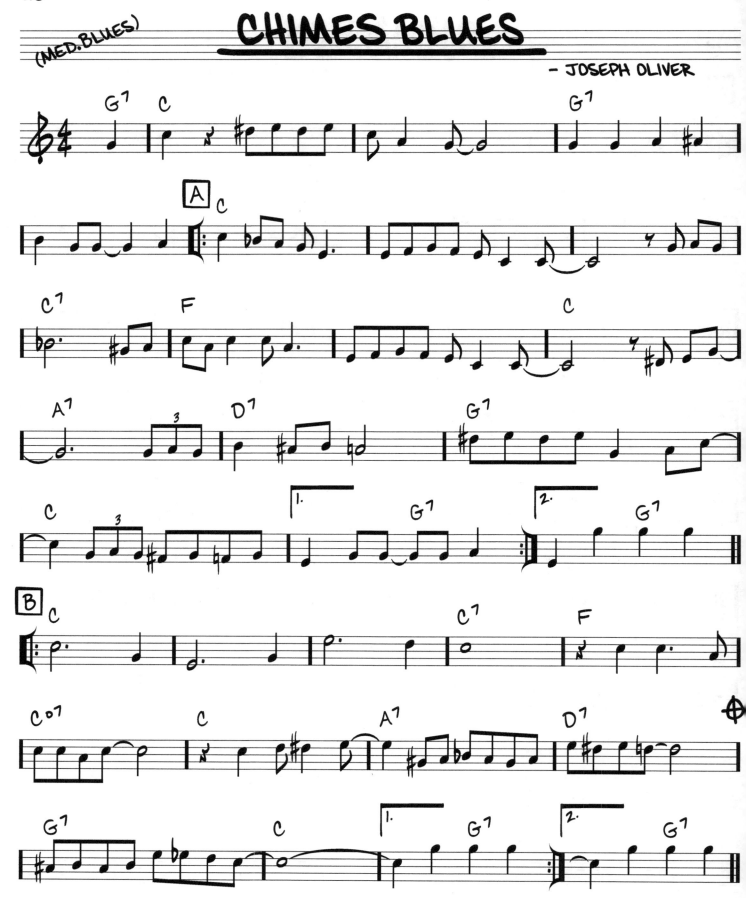

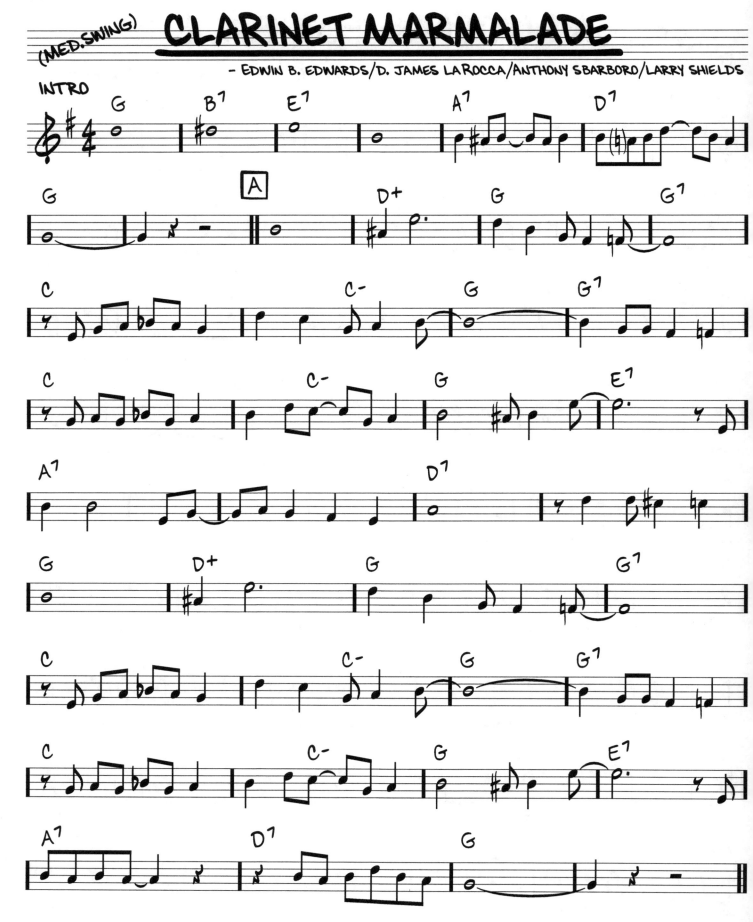

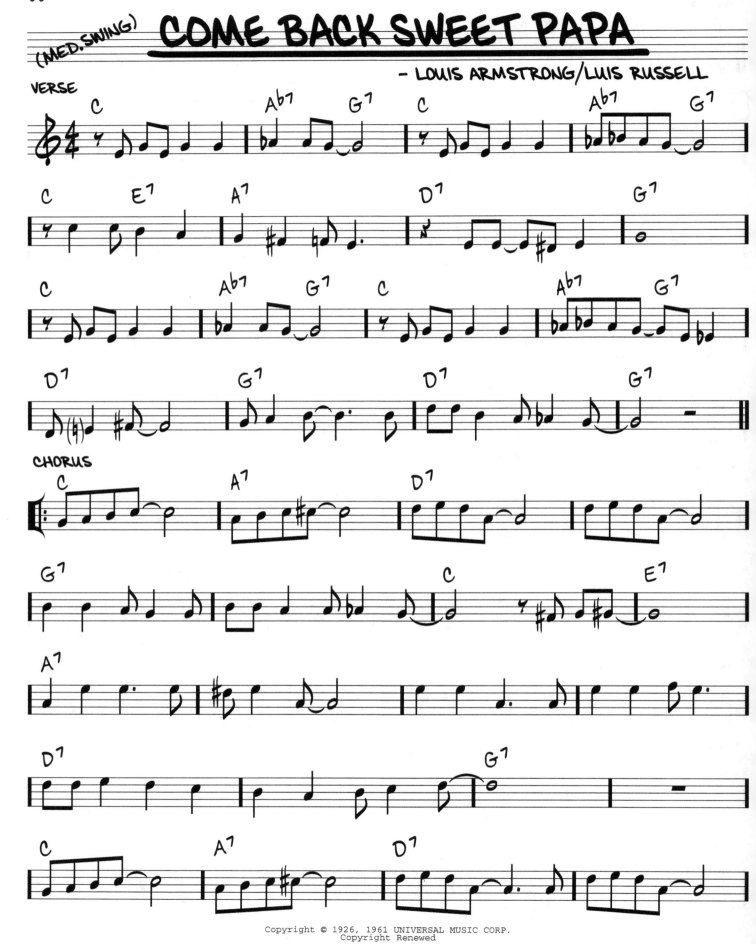

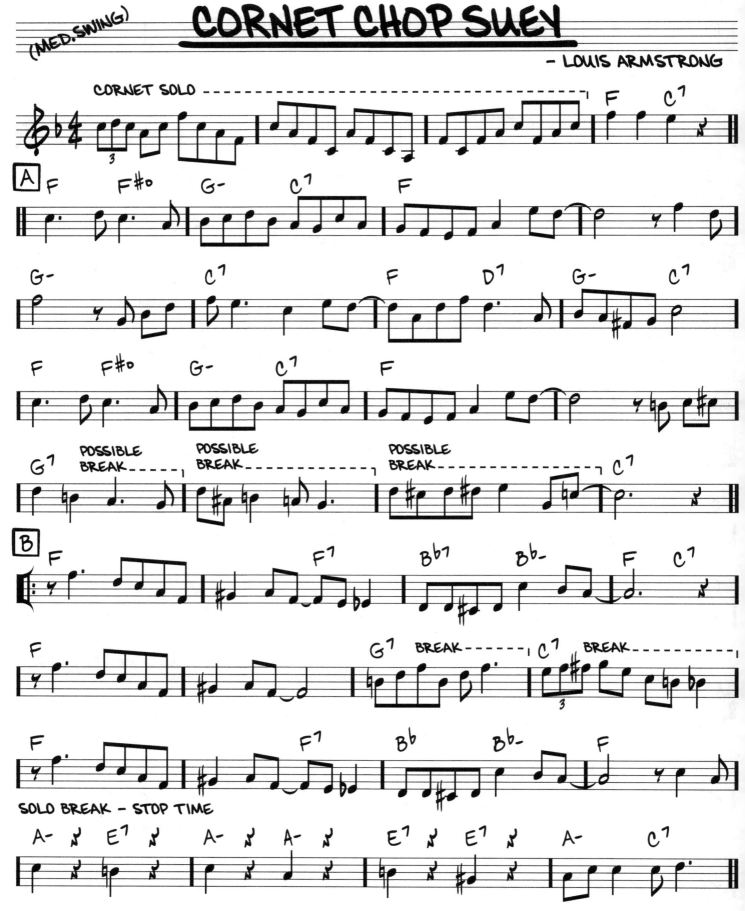

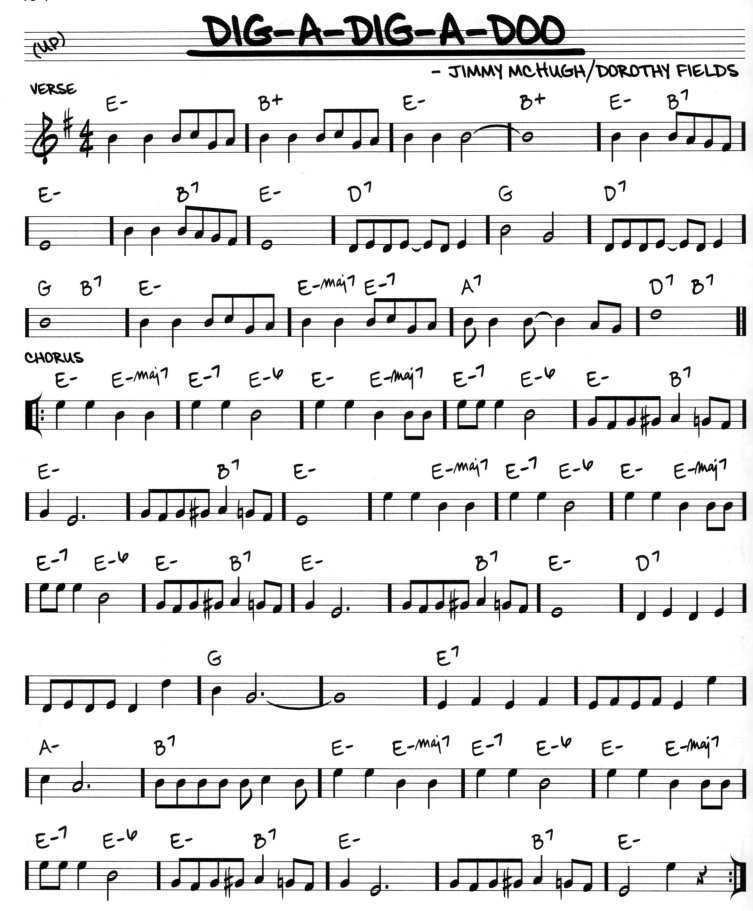

*MUGGSY SPANIER PLAYS INTRO ON $C\#o7$, STARTING ON G. EITHER CHORD, AS WELL AS VARIOUS STARTING NOTES, ARE POSSIBLE.

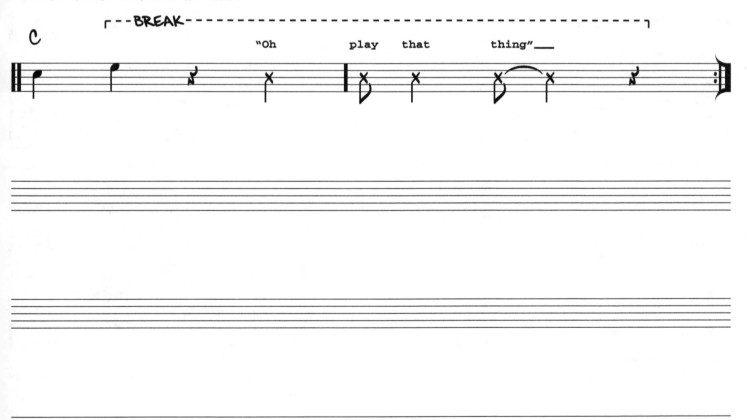

Down Home Rag

- Roger Lewis/Wilbur C. Sweatman

(up)

F (G-7 F/A Bb-6/G F D-7 G7 C7)

F (G-7 F/A Bb-6/G F D-7 G7 C7 F)

F6 ... G7 C7

F6 ... G7 C7 F

DOGFIGHT

F7 (Ab7 C- Ab7 F7 Eb Fo7 F7)

Bb (Bb7 Eb Eb-) C7 F7

Bb (Bb7 Eb Eb-) C F7 Bb

SOLOS USUALLY ON ONE CHORD
DOGFIGHT & TRIO OFTEN OMITTED

Copyright © 2010 by HAL LEONARD CORPORATION

THE FISH MAN
(LE MARCHAND DE POISSONS)

— FERNAD BONIFAY/SIDNEY BECHET/JESSIE CAVANAUGH

(MED. SWING)

Solos on C

© Copyright 1956 (Renewed) Editions Musicales Carrousel, Paris, France
TRO - Melody Trails, Inc., New York, controls all publication rights for the U.S.A. and Canada
International Copyright Secured
All Rights Reserved Including Public Performance For Profit
Used by Permission

FIVE FOOT TWO, EYES OF BLUE
(HAS ANYBODY SEEN MY GIRL?)

(MED. BRIGHT)

– JOE YOUNG/SAM LEWIS/RAY HENDERSON

Five foot two, eyes of blue, but oh, what those five
foot could do.__ Has an-y-bod-y seen my girl?__
Turned up nose, turned down hose, A flap-per? Yes sir,
one of those.__ Has an-y-bod-y seen my
girl?__ Now if you run in-to a five foot two
cov-ered with fur,__ Dia-mond rings and all those things,
bet-cha' life it is-n't her.__ But could she love,
could she woo? Could she, could she, could she coo?__ Has
an-y-bod-y seen my girl?__

© 1925 LEO FEIST, INC.
© Renewed 1953 WAROCK CORP., EMI FEIST CATALOG INC. and RAY HENDERSON MUSIC CO. in the United States
All Rights for EMI FEIST CATALOG INC. Administered by EMI FEIST CATALOG INC. (Publishing) and ALFRED MUSIC (Print)
All Rights for the Sam Lewis and Ray Henderson shares in the British Reversionary Territories Administered by REDWOOD MUSIC LTD.

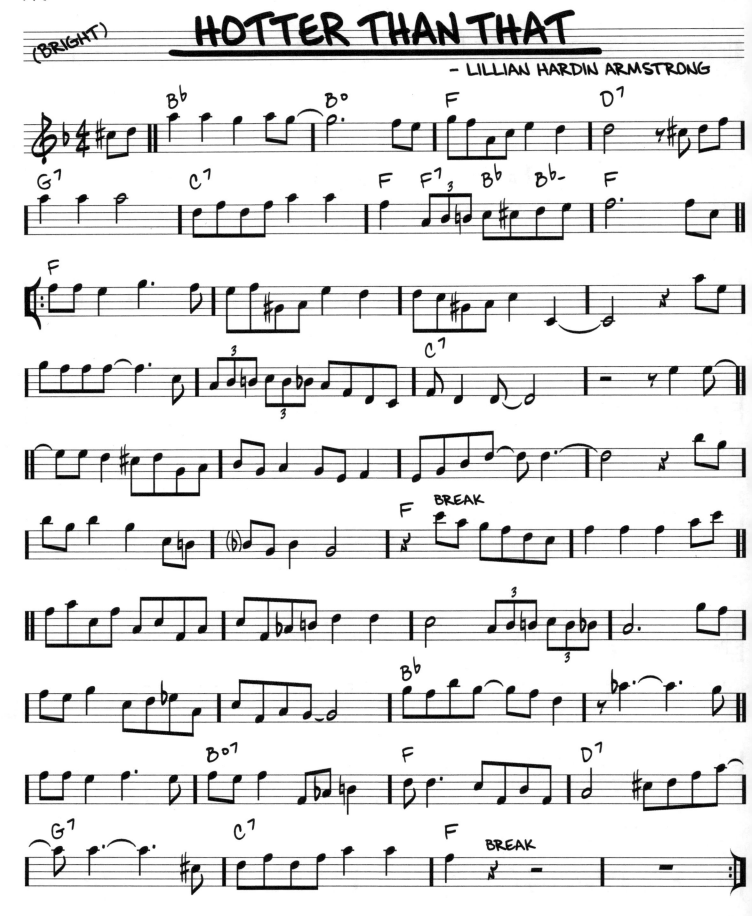

(BRIGHT) I Can't Give You Anything But Love

— JIMMY McHUGH/DOROTHY FIELDS

153

I can't give you an-y-thing but love,___ Ba-by.___

That's the on-ly thing I've plen-ty of,___ Ba - by.

Dream a - while,_ scheme a - while,_ we're sure to find,___

Hap - pi - ness___ and I guess,_ All those things you've al - ways pined for.

Gee, I'd like to see you look-ing swell,___ Ba - by.

Dia - mond brace - lets Wool - worth does-n't sell, Ba - by.

Till that luck - y day, you know darned well, Ba - by,___

I can't give you an - y - thing but love.___

© 1928 (Renewed 1956) COTTON CLUB PUBLISHING and ALDI MUSIC
All Rights for COTTON CLUB PUBLISHING Controlled and Administered by EMI APRIL MUSIC INC.
Print Rights for ALDI MUSIC in the U.S. Controlled and Administered by HAPPY ASPEN MUSIC LLC c/o SHAPIRO, BERNSTEIN & CO., INC.

(BRIGHT) I'M GONNA SIT RIGHT DOWN AND WRITE MYSELF A LETTER

- JOE YOUNG/FRED E. AHLERT

I'm gon-na sit right down and write my-self a let-ter,____ And make be-lieve it came from you.____ I'm gon-na write words, oh, so sweet,____ They're gon-na knock me off my feet.____ A lot of kiss-es on the bot-tom, I'll be glad I got 'em,____ I'm gon-na smile and say, "I hope you're feel-ing bet-ter",____ And close with love the way you do.____ I'm gon-na sit right down and write my-self a let-ter,____ And make be-lieve it came from you.____ (I'm gon-na)

© 1935 CHAPPELL & CO.
© Renewed 1962 RYTVOC, INC., PENCIL MARK MUSIC, AZURE PEARL MUSIC, BEEPING GOOD MUSIC and DAVID AHLERT MUSIC
All Rights for PENCIL MARK MUSIC Administered by BMG RIGHTS MANAGEMENT (US) LLC
All Rights for AZURE PEARL MUSIC, BEEPING GOOD MUSIC and DAVID AHLERT MUSIC Administered by BLUEWATER MUSIC SERVICES CORP.

*MELODY TO BRIDGE IS OFTEN PLAYED TWO BEATS EARLIER, BEGINNING WITH A PICKUP, AS PER CHICAGO RHYTHM KINGS 1928.

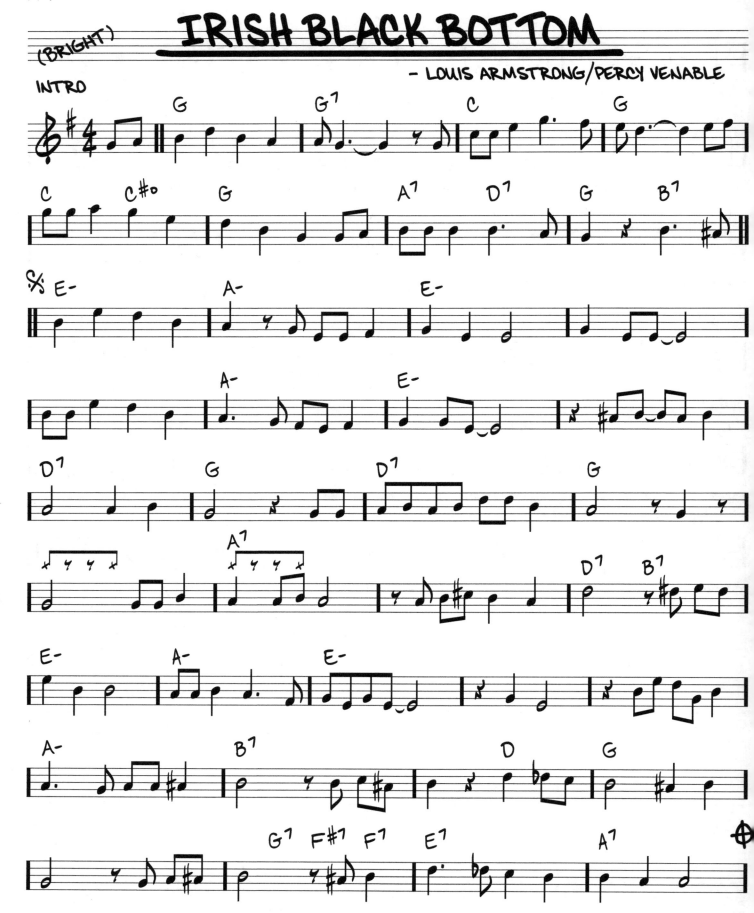

THE JAZZ-ME BLUES

– TOM DELANEY

(MED.)

1. Down in Lou - si - an - a in that sun - ny clime,__ they
2. Ev - 'ry - bod - y now a days__ does that dance.__ You'd

play a class of mu - sic that is sup - er fine.__ And it
bet - ter learn to jazz now while you've got the chance._____ This

makes no dif - fer - ence if it's__ rain or shine,__ you can
pleas - ing synch - o - pa - tion has__ come to stay.__ Now__

BREAK -

hear that jazz - in' mu - sic play - ing all the time.__ It
all you've got to do is just to jazz a - way.__ So

sounds so pe - cu - li - ar 'cause the mu - sic's queer,__
when you hear that band__ play - ing at the ball,__

how its sweet vi - bra - tion seems to fill the air.__
grab your gal and do your stuff a - round the hall.__ With__

Then to you the whole world seems to be in rhyme,__ you want
noth - ing on your mind but mu - sic and your brown,__ on - ly

BREAK -

noth - ing else but jazz - in', jazz - in' all the time.__
wait - ing for the time so you can jazz her 'round.__

Copyright © 2010 by HAL LEONARD CORPORATION

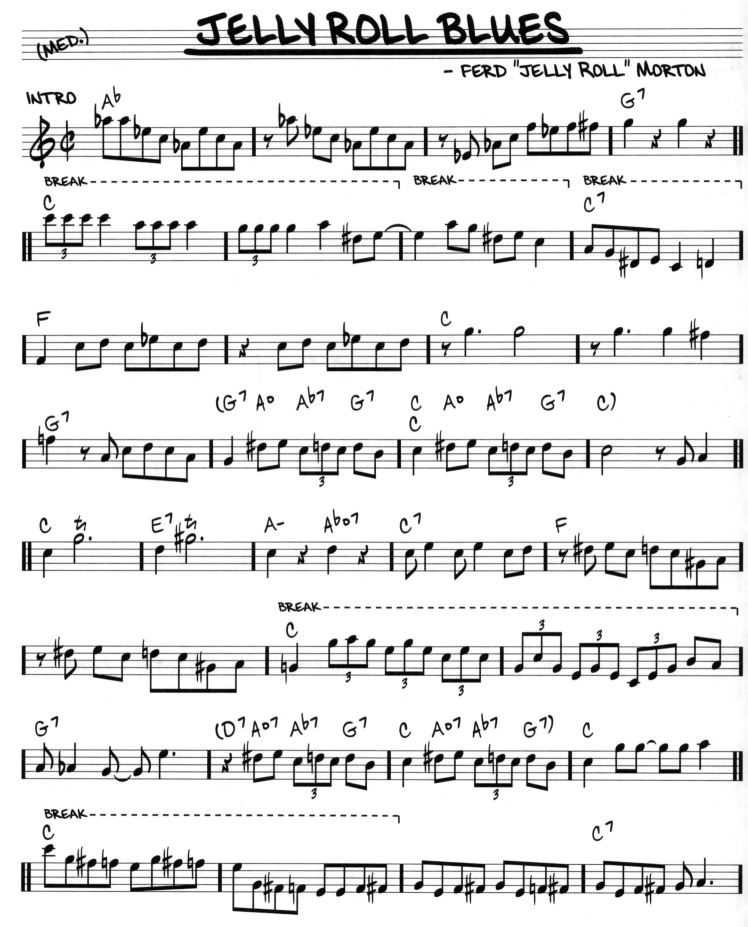

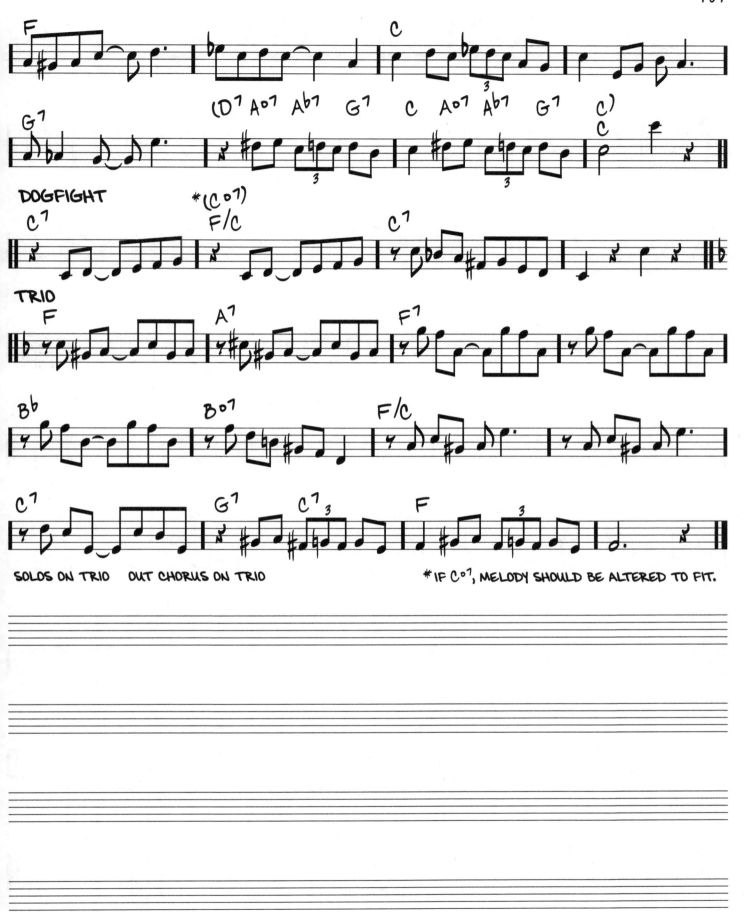

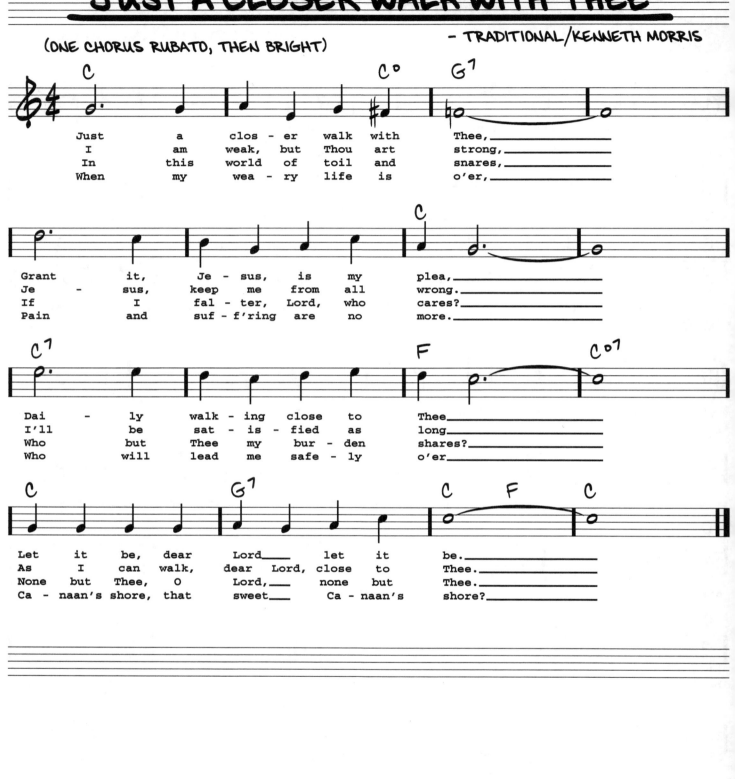

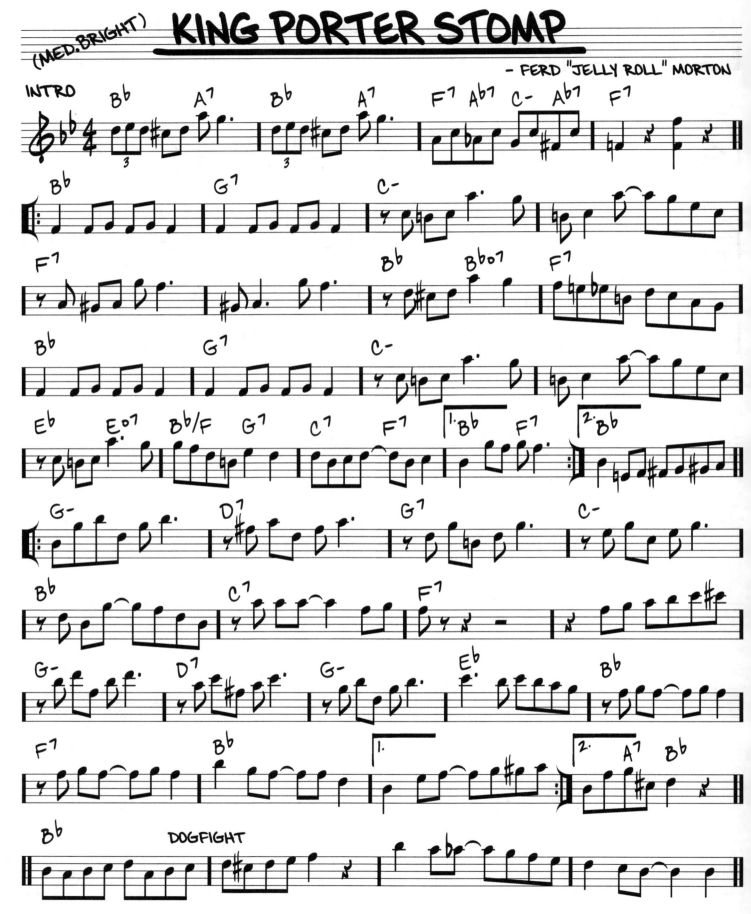

CHORUS

THE LONESOME ROAD

— AFRICAN-AMERICAN SPIRITUAL

(MED.)

Look down, look down that lone - some road___ Be -

fore you tra - vel on.___ Look

up, look up and seek your mak - er 'Fore

Gab - riel blows his horn.___

Wear - y tot - in' such a load.

Trud - gin' down___ the lone - some road. Look

down, look down that lone - some road___ Be -

fore you tra - vel on.___ (Look)

Copyright © 2010 by HAL LEONARD CORPORATION

*SOME INSTRUMENTAL VERSIONS (E.G. BIX) EXTEND THE VERSE TO 16 BARS BY INSERTING THE FIRST 4 BARS AT THIS POINT.

Copyright © 1927 by Razaf Music Co. and Alfred Music
Copyright Renewed
All Rights for Razaf Music Co. Administered by PRIMARY WAVE WHITE

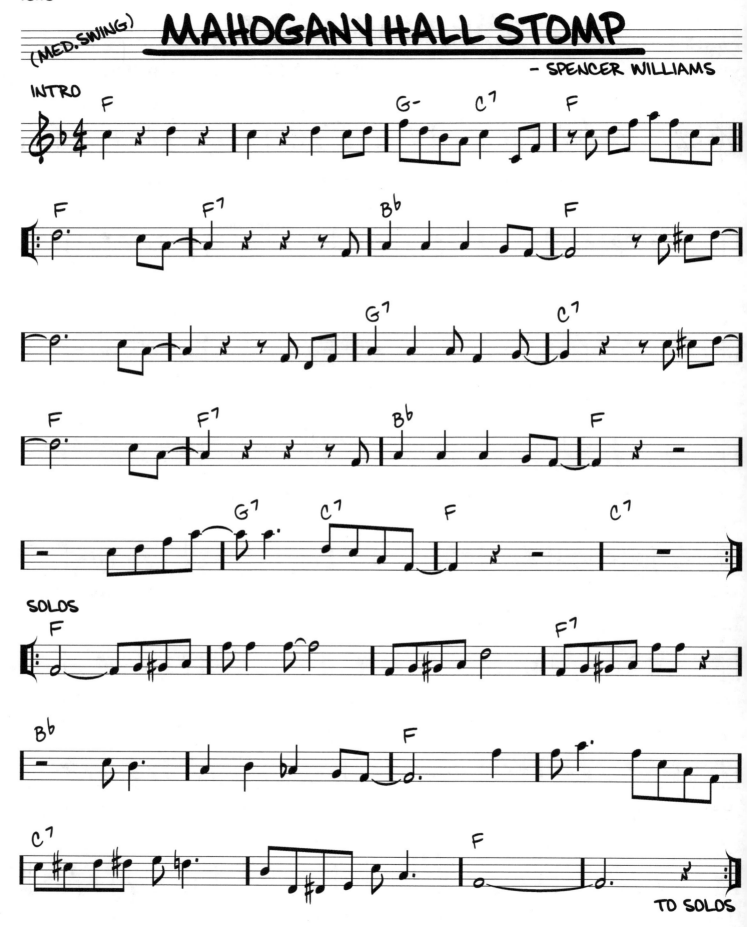

TPT. GENERALLY PLAYS THIS FIGURE FOR LAST SOLO CHORUS.

Makin' Whoopee!

(MED. SWING)

— Gus Kahn/Walter Donaldson

Ev-'ry time I hear that march from Loh-en-grin,__ I'm al-ways on the out-side__ look-in' in.__ May-be that is why I see the fun-ny side,__ when I see a fall-en broth-er take a bride.__ Wed-dings make a lot of peo-ple sad, but if you're not the groom you're not so bad. An-oth-er

bride,____ an-oth-er June,____ an-oth-er sun — ny hon-ey-moon,____ an-oth-er sea-son,____ an-oth-er rea-son____ for mak-in' whoo-pee!____

year,____ or may-be less,____ what's this I hear?____ Well, can't you guess?____ She feels neg-lect-ed,____ and he's sus-pect-ed____ of mak-in' whoo-pee!____ She sits a-lone____ most ev-'ry night,____

A lot of shoes,____ a lot of rice,____ the groom is nerv-ous,____ he an-swers twice.____ It's real-ly

he does-n't phone her, he does-n't write.____ He say he's

Copyright © 1928 (Renewed) by Donaldson Publishing Co., Dreyer Music Co. and Gilbert Keyes Music Company
All Rights for Dreyer Music Co. Administered by Larry Spier, Inc., New York
All Rights for Gilbert Keyes Music Company Administered by WB Music Corp.

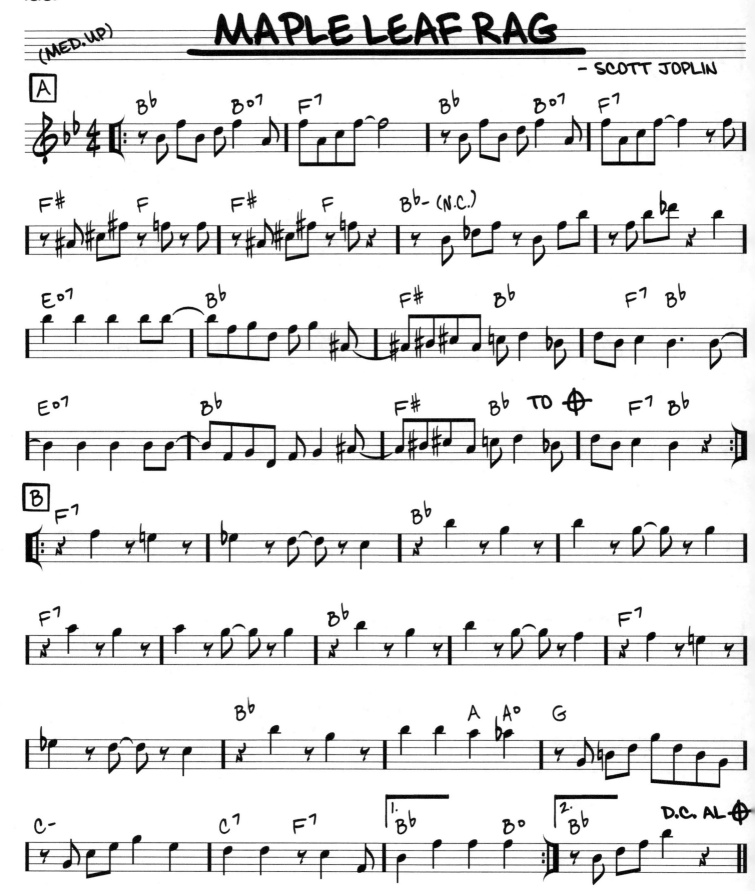

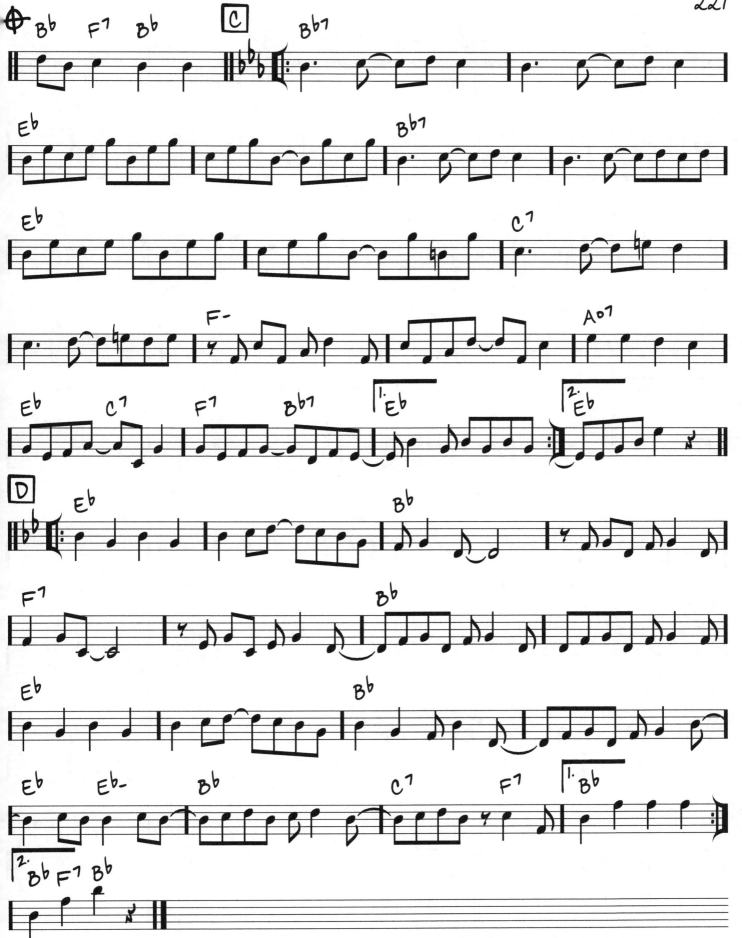

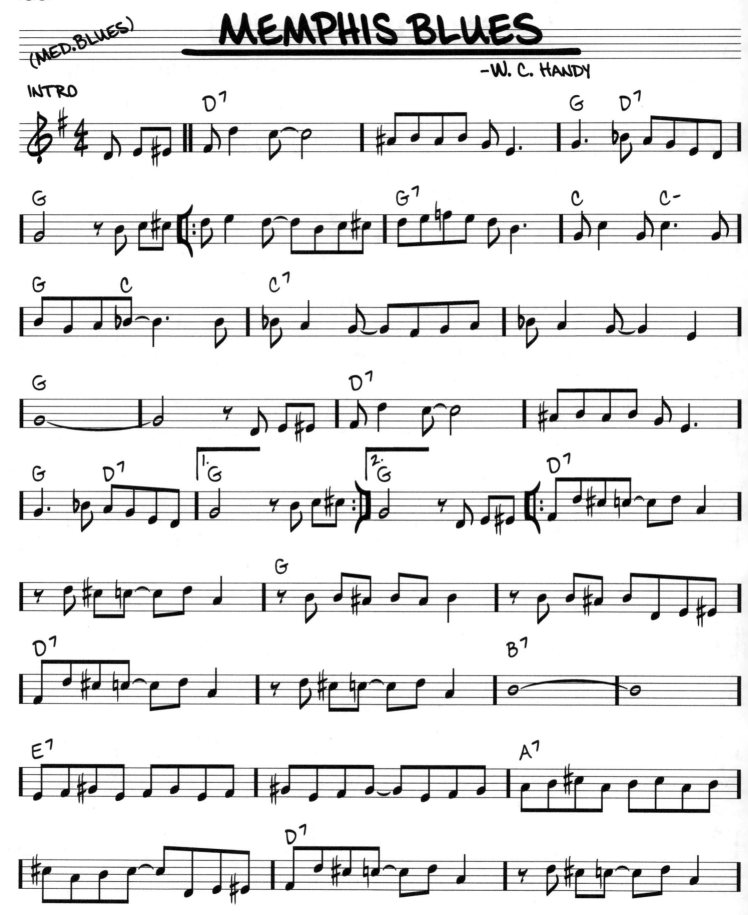

*FOR INSTRUMENTAL VERSION PLAY THIS MEASURE AS FOLLOWS:

Additional Lyrics:

Lazily the brook like a silvery stream
Ripples in the light of the moon
And a song afar fades as in a dream
In this night that will end too soon

Dearest, why so sad, why the downcast eyes
And your lovely head bent so low
Oh, I mustn't speak, thought I'd love to say
That you've stolen my heart away

Promise me my love, as the dawn appears
And the darkness turns into light
That you'll cherish dear, through the passing years
This most beautiful Moscow Night

© Copyright 1961 (Renewed) Tyler Music Ltd., London, England
TRO - Melody Trails, Inc., New York, controls all publication rights for the U.S.A. and Canada

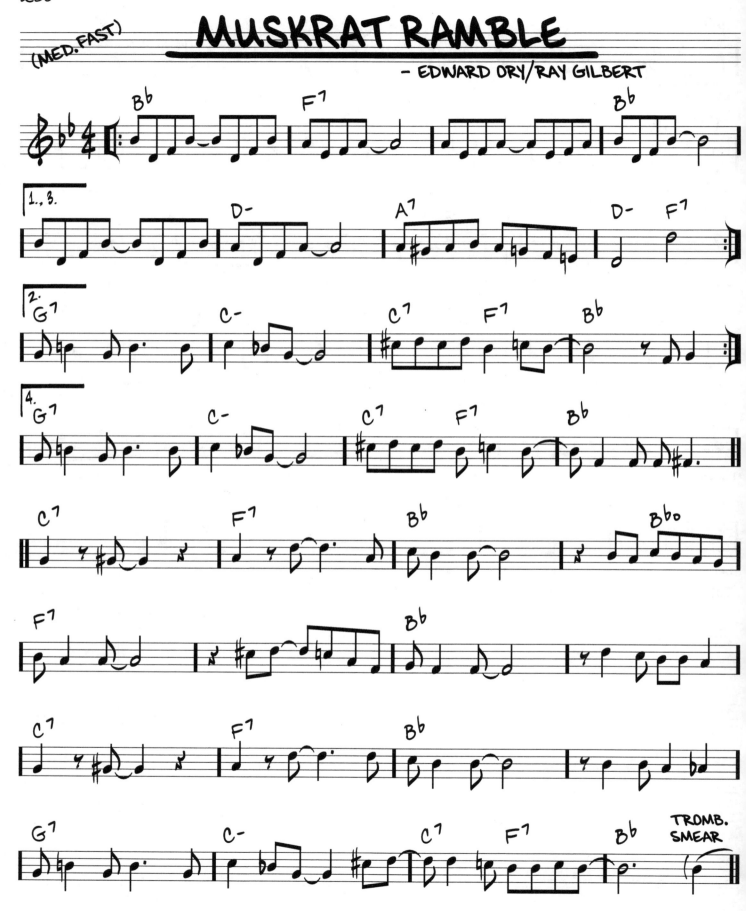

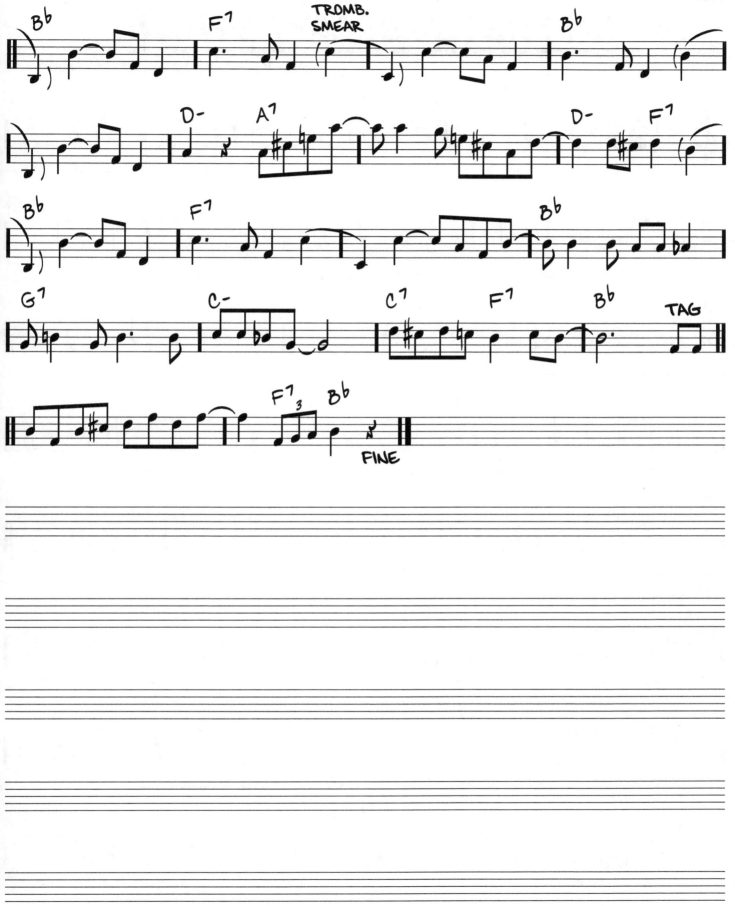

Extra Lyrics

BOY:
My baby's no Crosby fan
Dick Tracy is not her man
My baby just care for me
My baby don't care for Mr. Tibbits
She'd rather have me...around to kibbitz
Roy Rogers is not her style...and even Clark Gable's smile
Is something that she can't see
I wonder what's wrong with baby
My baby just cares for me

GIRL:
My baby don't care for shows
My baby don't care for clothes
My baby just cares for me.
My baby don't care for cars and races
My baby don't care for high-toned places.
Liz Taylor is not his style and even Lana Turner's smile
Is something he can't see.
My baby don't care who knows it
My baby just cares for me.

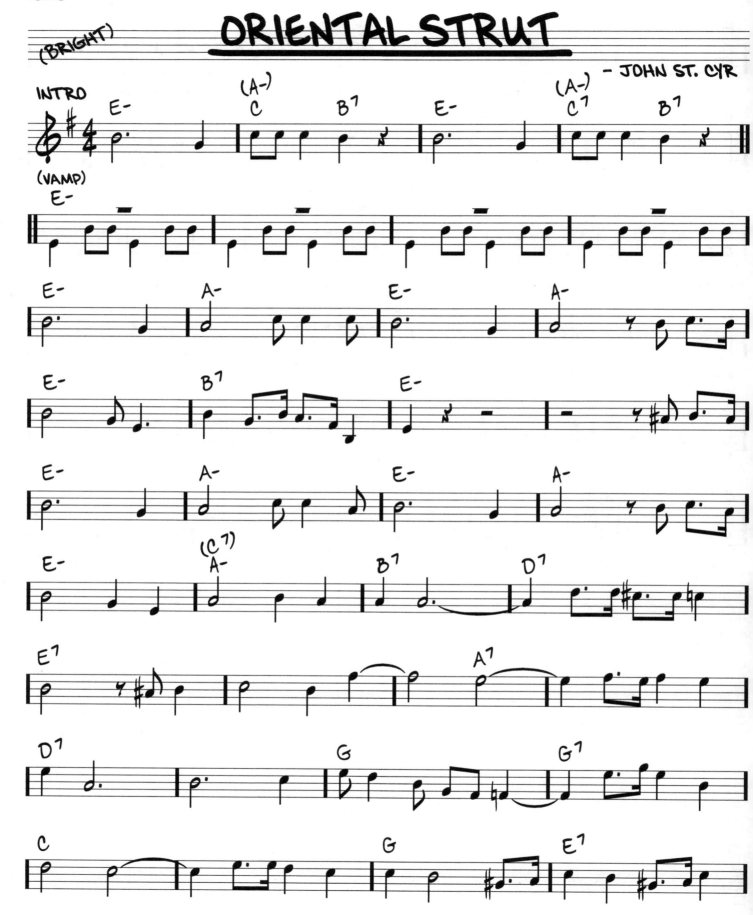

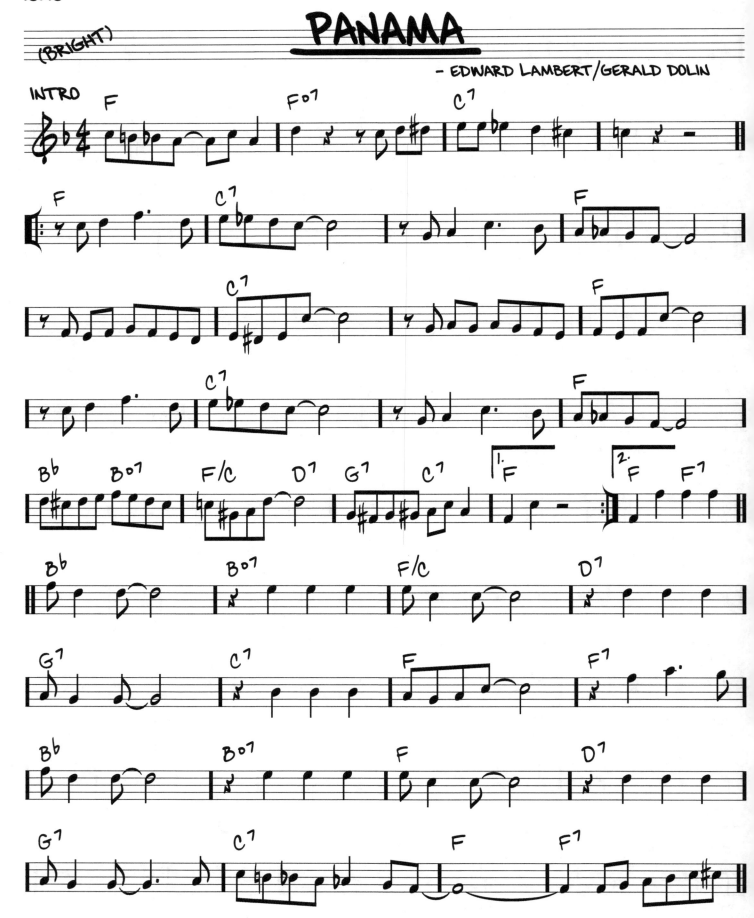

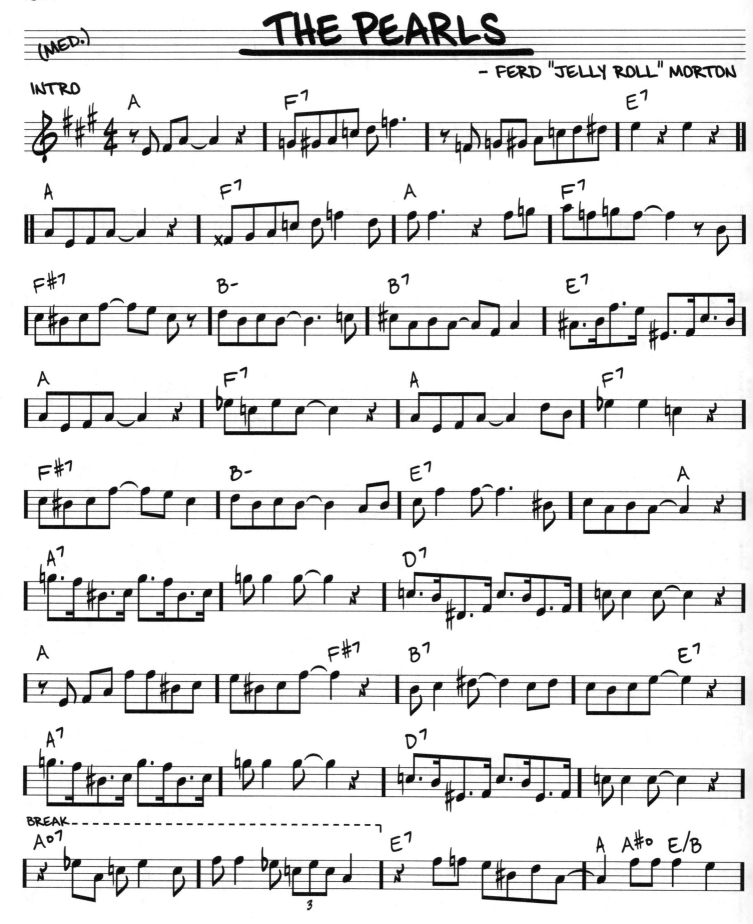

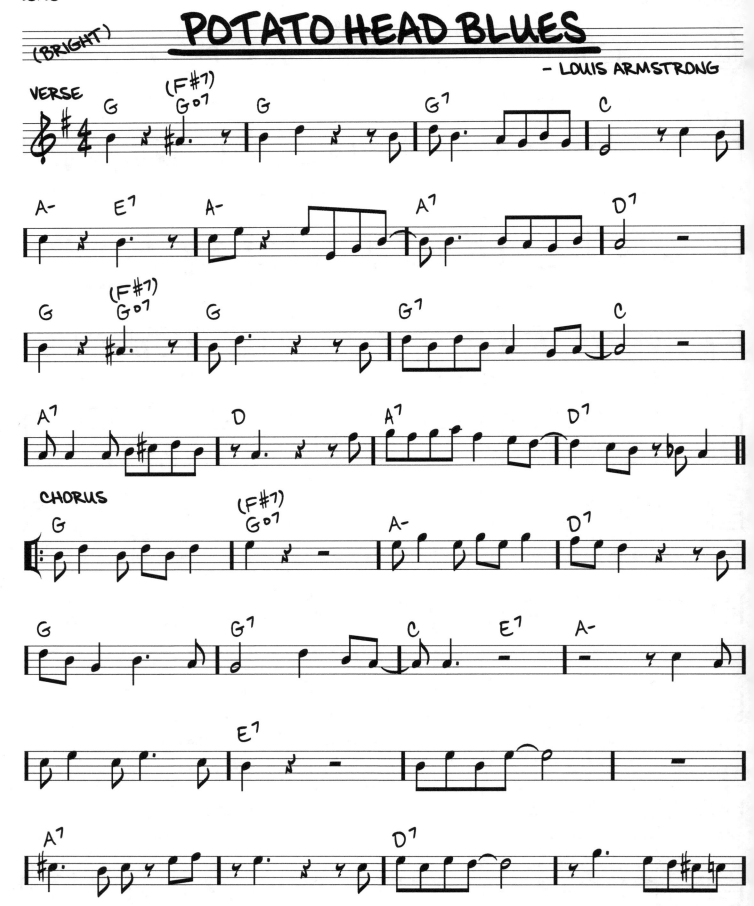

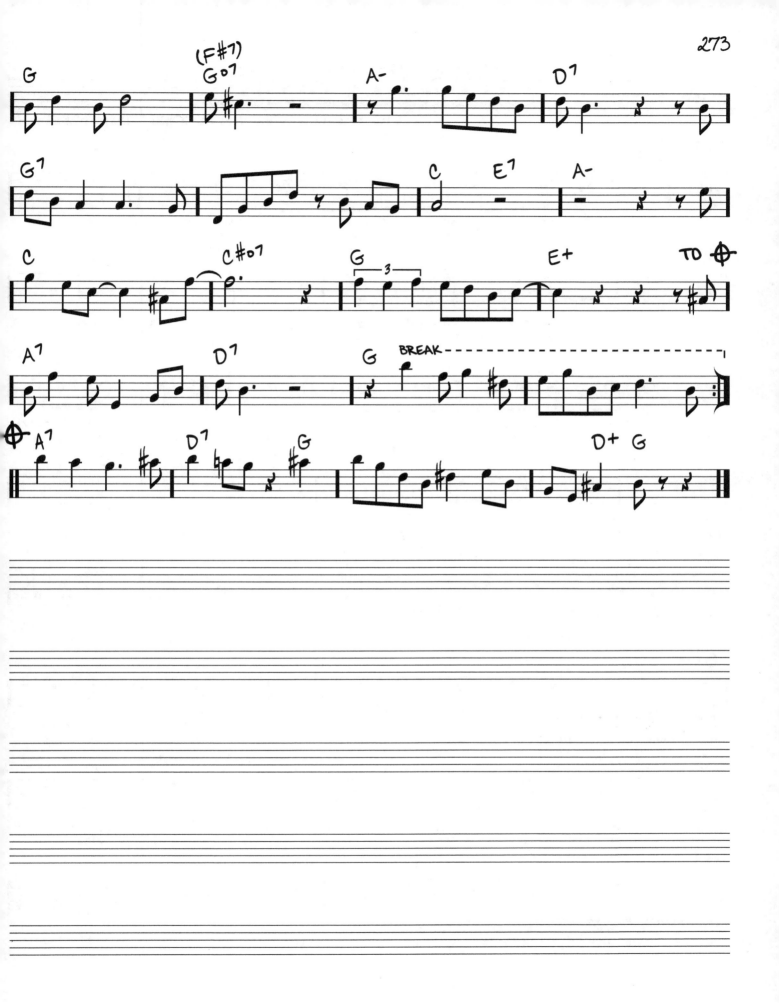

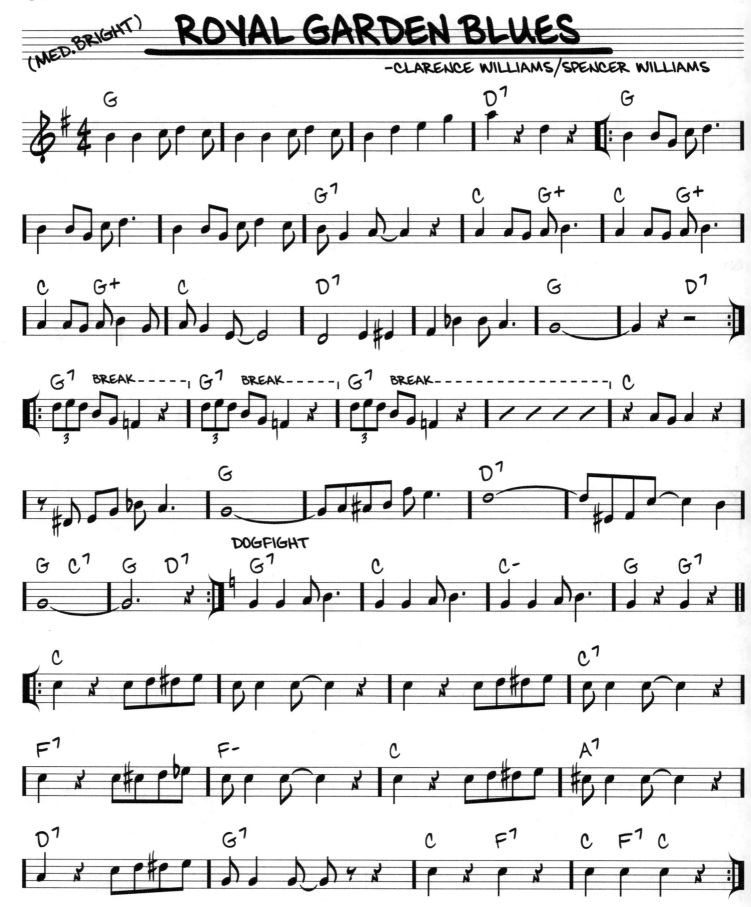

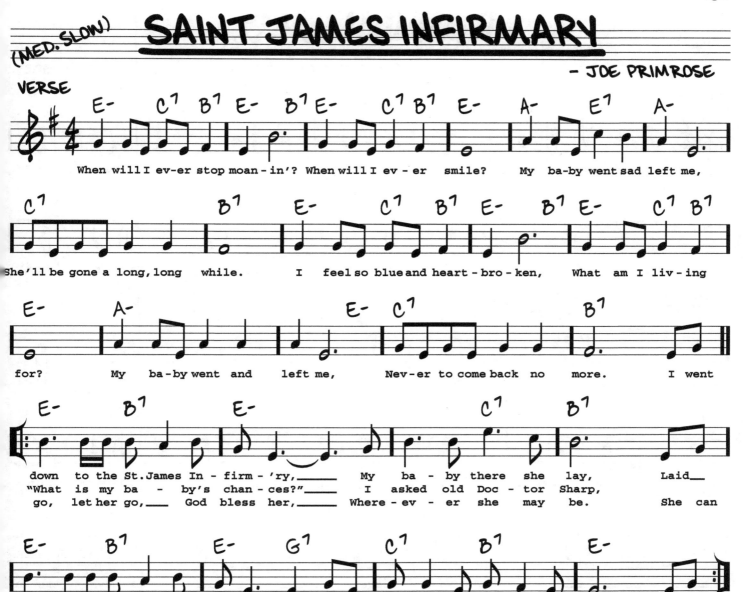

1. I went down to St. James Infirm'ry.
   All was still as night,
   My gal was on the table,
   Stretched out so pale, so white.
     Through she treated me mean and lowdown,
     Somehow I didn't care,
     My soul is sick and weary,
     I hope we meet again up there.

   CHORUS:
   Let her go, let her go, God bless her,
   Wherever she may be,
   She can hunt this wide world over,
   But she'll never find a man like me.

2. Sixteen coal-black horses,
   Hitched to a rubber-tired hack,
   Carried seven girls to the graveyard,
   And brought only six of them back.
     Now when I die, please bury me,
     In my milk-white Stetson hat,
     With a five-doller gold piece on my watch chain,
     So they'll know I died standin' pat.

3. Six poker dealers for pall bearers,
   Let a whore sing my funeral song,
   With a red hot band just beatin' it out,
   Raisin' hell as we roll along.
     Now I may be drowned in the ocean,
     May be killed by a cannonball,
     But let me tell you buddy,
     A woman was the cause of it all.

Copyright © 2010 by HAL LEONARD CORPORATION

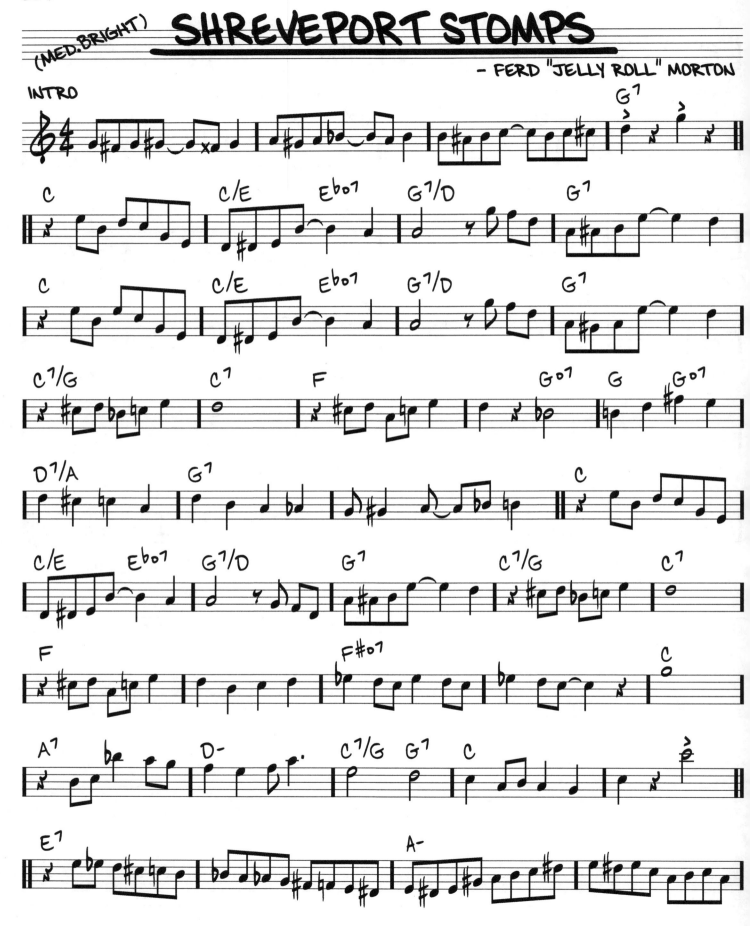

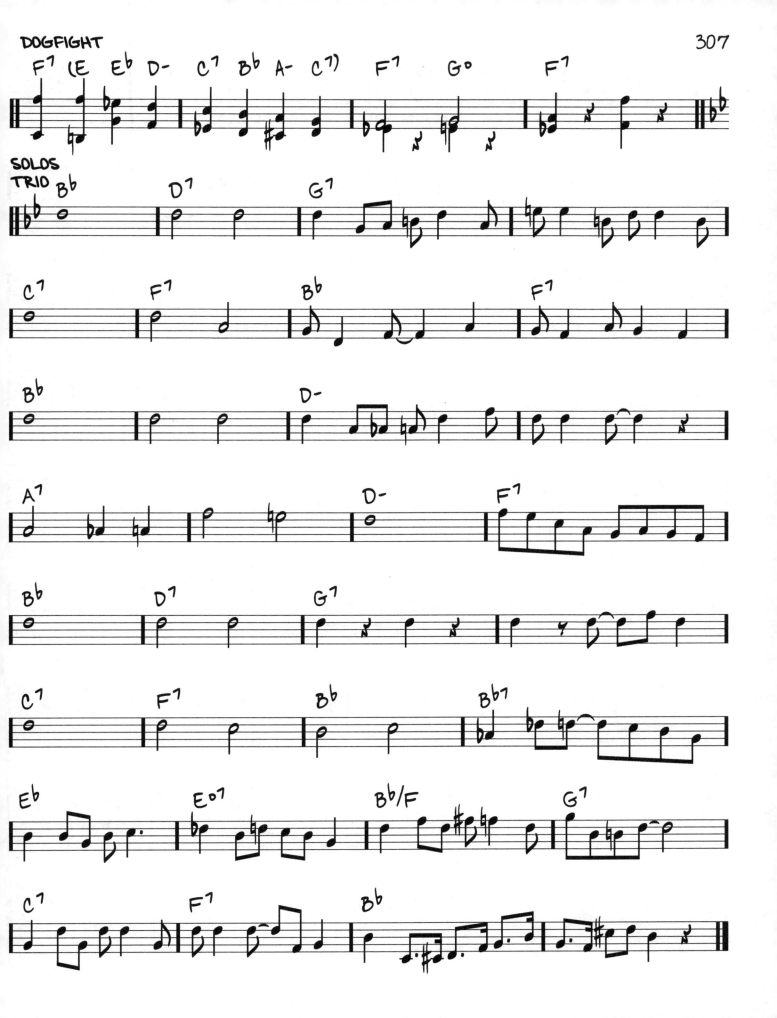

(MED.) SINGIN' THE BLUES TILL MY DADDY COMES HOME

– SAM M. LEWIS/JOE YOUNG/CON CONRAD/J. RUSSELL ROBINSON

Oh, I'm just sing-in' the blues_____ till my dad-dy comes home;_____

_____ the mean-est feel-in' pur-sues_____ since he left me a - lone._____

_____ For ev - 'ry blue strain puts new pain right in-to my heart,_____

_____ and I just sigh at the cry - in' part._____ It

sure gets your nerves_____ when you hear your-self moan._____ If I got

all I de - serves,_____ I would-n't be_____ here all a - lone; I would-n't

watch all night, and sit by the win-dow with a can - dle - light;_____

sing-in' the blues_____ till my dad-dy comes home._____ (Oh, I'm just)

Copyright © 2010 by HAL LEONARD CORPORATION

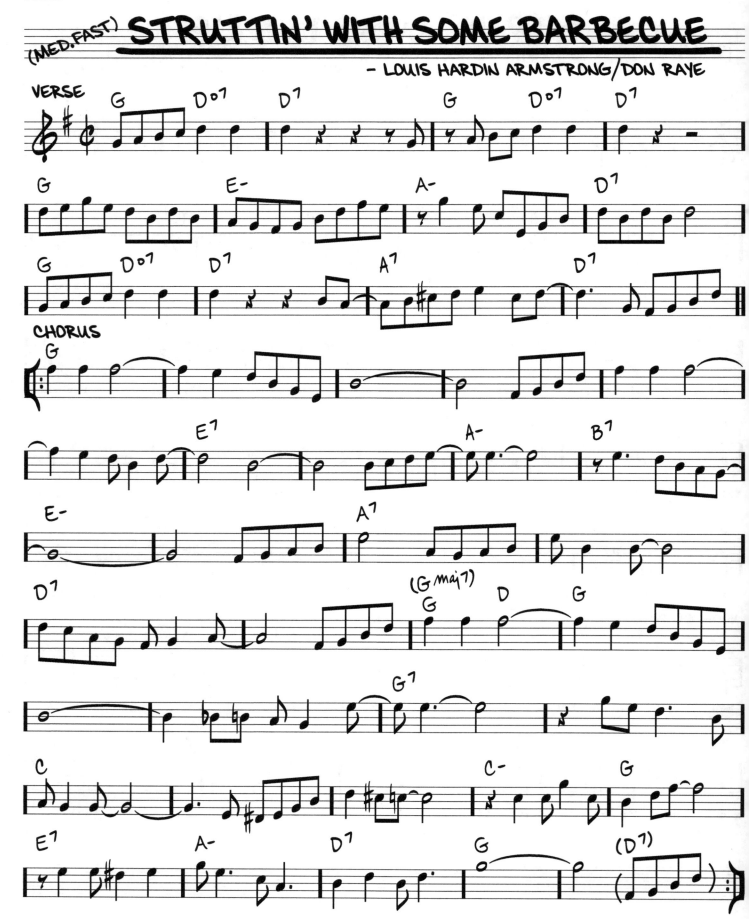

Additional Lyrics:

And if I should get a feeling
I wanna dance upon the ceiling
'Tain't nobody's business if I do

If I stay out all night
Spend all my money, well that's all right
'Tain't nobody's business if I do

If I let my best companion,
Drive me right in the canyon,
'Tain't nobody's business if I do

Well, I won't call no copper,
If I'm beat up by my papa,
'Tain't nobody's business if I do

There, I'd rather my man was hittin' me,
Than to jump right up and quittin' me,
'Tain't nobody's business if I do

If my daddy got no money,
And I play bridge all night, honey,
'Tain't nobody's business if I do

If my friend ain't got no money,
And I say, "Take all mine, honey",
'Tain't nobody's business if I do

If I give him my last nickel,
And it leaves me in a pickle,
'Tain't nobody's business if I do

Copyright © 2010 by HAL LEONARD CORPORATION

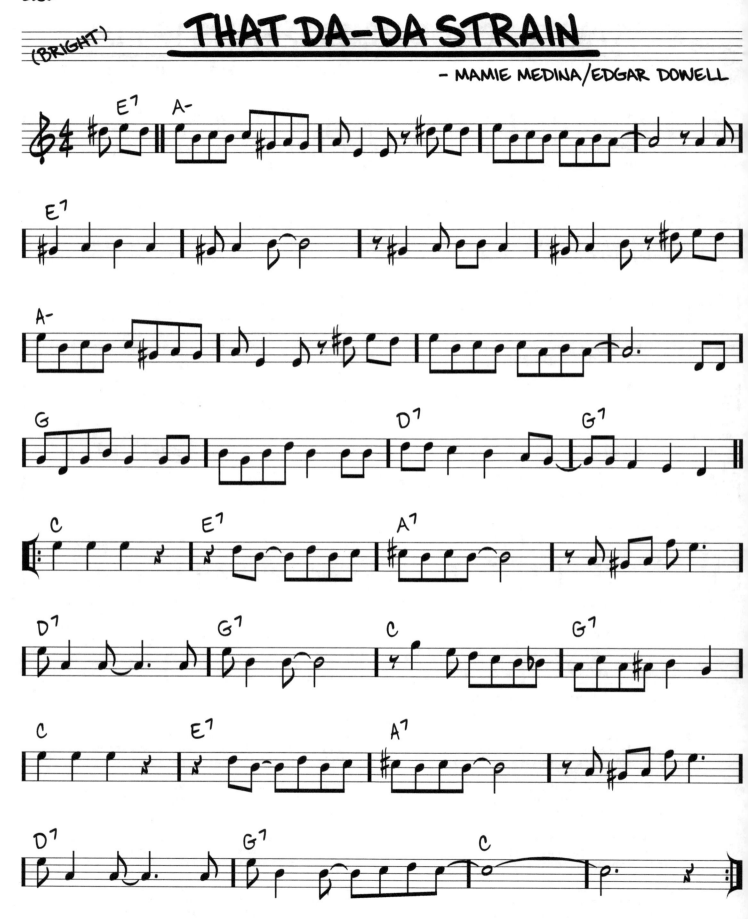

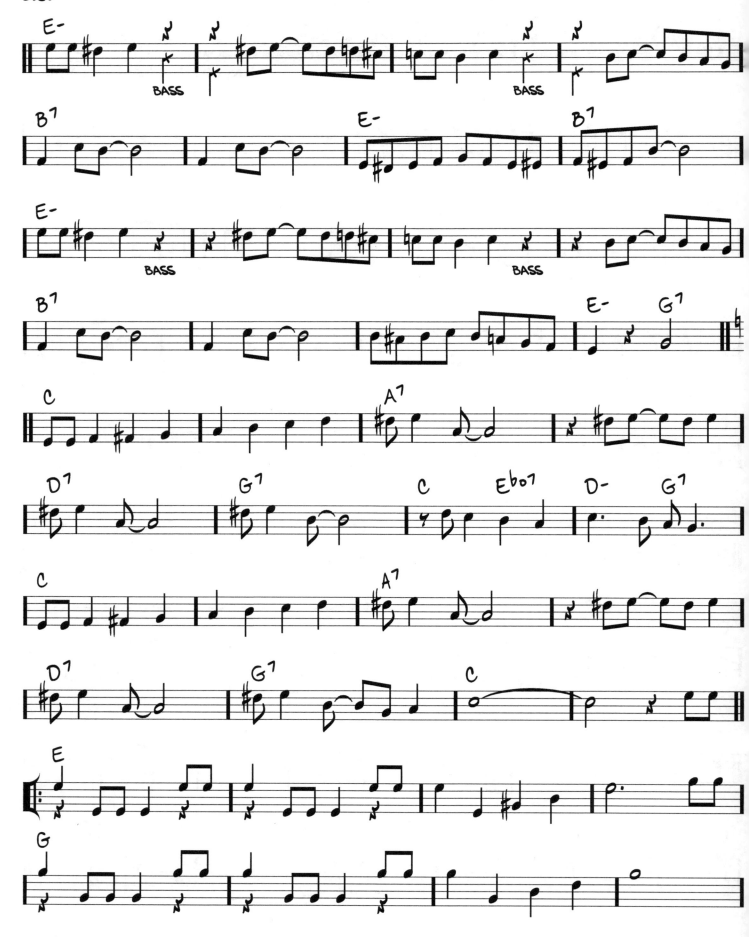

Extra Choruses

3. There's a change in your manner and a change in your way;
   there was time once when you was okay.
   You once said you saved ev'ry kiss for my sake;
   now you're giving all the girls an even break.
   I'm gonna send out invitations to the men I know,
   'cause you're gettin' colder than an Eskimo.
   I must have my lovin' or I'll fade away,
   there'll be some changes made today,
   There'll be some changes made.

4. For there's a change in your manner, there's a change in your style,
   and here of late you never wear a smile.
   You don't seem to act like a real love should,
   you can't thrill your mamma if you're made of wood.
   I gotta have a man who loves me like a real live Sheik,
   with a tasty kiss that lingers for a week...
   I'm not over sixty, so it's time to say:
   There'll be some changes made today,
   There'll be some changes made.

5. For there's a change in your squeezin', there's a change in your kiss,
   it used to have a kick that I now miss.
   You'd set me on fire when you used to tease,
   now each time you call I just sit there and freeze.
   You had a way of making love that made a hit with me,
   one time you could thrill me but it's plain to see:
   You're not so ambitious as you used to be.
   There'll be some changes made by me,
   There'll be some changes made.

6. For there's a change in the weather, there's a change in the sea,
   from now on there'll be a change in me.
   I'm tired of working all of my life,
   I'm gonna grab a rich husband and be his wife.
   I'm going to ride around in a big limousine,
   wear fancy clothes and put on plenty of steam.
   No more tired puppies, will I treat you mean,
   there'll be some changes made today,
   There'll be some changes made.

7. For there's a change in your manner, there's a change in your smile,
   from now on you can't be worth my while.
   I'm right here to tell you with you I'm through,
   your brand of lovin' will never do.
   I'm gettin' tired of eating just butter and bread,
   I could enjoy a few pork chops instead.
   You know variety is the spice of life they say,
   there'll be some changes made today (I'll get mine!),
   There'll be some changes made.

TIGER RAG
(HOLD THAT TIGER)

— Harry DeCosta/Original Dixieland Jazz Band

Copyright © 2010 by HAL LEONARD CORPORATION

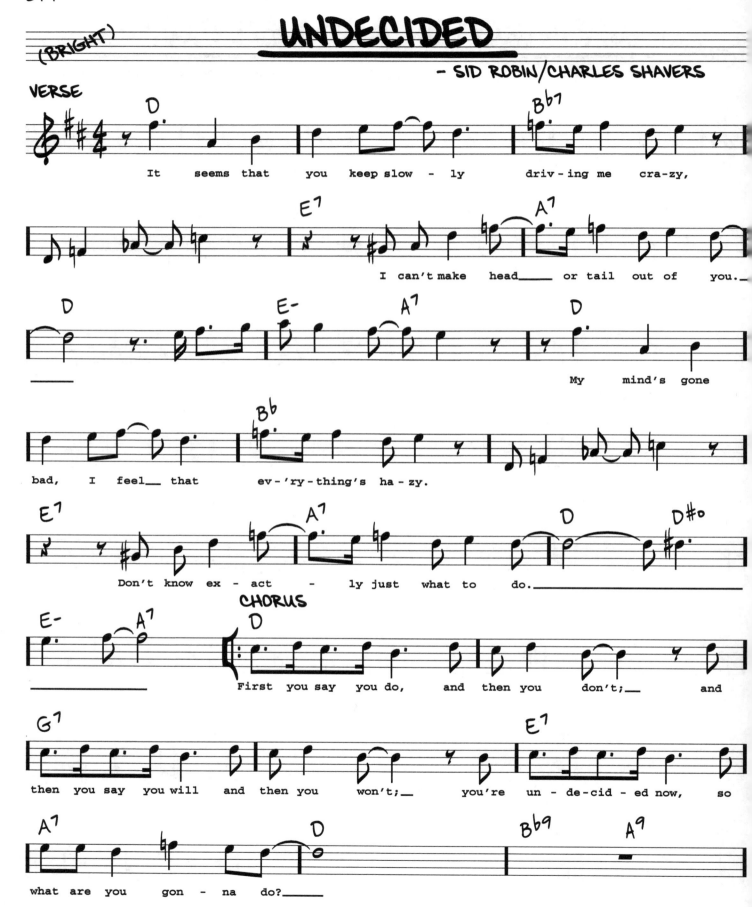

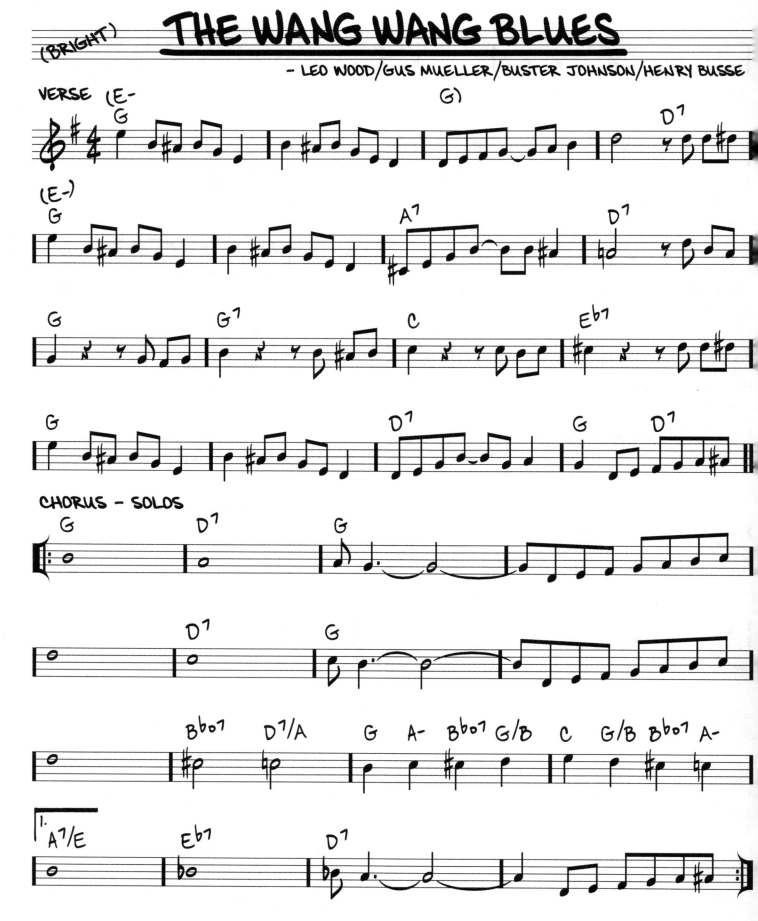

'Way Down Yonder In New Orleans

(BRIGHT)

- HENRY CREAMER/J. TURNER LAYTON

'Way down yon - der in New Or - leans,___ in the land___ of
dream - y scenes,___ There's a gar - den of E - den, that's what I mean.___
Cre - ole ba - bies with flash - ing eyes,___ soft - ly whis - per with
ten - der sighs:___ "Stop! Oh! Won't you give your la - dy fair___
a lit - tle smile?" Stop! You bet your life you'll lin - ger there
a lit - tle while. There is heav - en right
They've got an - gels right
here on earth,___ with those beau - ti - ful queens,
here on earth,___ wear - ing lit - tle blue jeans,
'Way down yon - der in New Or - leans.

Copyright © 2010 by HAL LEONARD CORPORATION

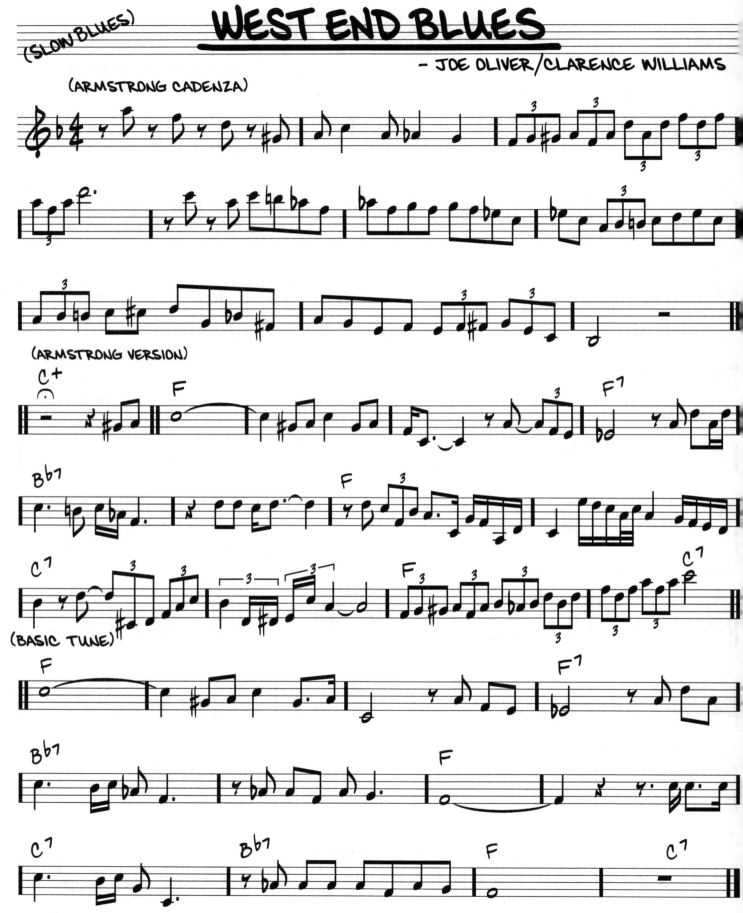

WHEN MY BABY SMILES AT ME

(MED.)

- HARRY VON TILZER/ANDREW B. STERLING/BILL MUNRO/TED LEWIS

For when my ba-by smiles at me my heart goes

roam-ing to par-a-dise. And when my

ba-by smiles at me there's such a

won-der-ful light in her eyes. The kind of

light that means just love, the kind of

love that brings sweet har-mon-y I

sigh. I cry. It's just a glimpse of heav-en when my

ba-by smiles at me. (For when my)

Copyright © 2010 by HAL LEONARD CORPORATION

2. Oh, when they come, on Judgement Day,
   Oh, when they come, on Judgement Day,
   Lord, I want to be in that number
   When they come on Judgement Day.

3. When Gabriel blows, that golden horn,
   When Gabriel blows, that golden horn,
   Lord, I want to be in that number
   When Gabriel blows, that golden horn.

4. When they go through them Pearly Gates,
   When they go through them Pearly Gates,
   Lord, I want to be in that number
   When they go through them Pearly Gates.

5. Oh, when they ring them silver bells,
   Oh, when they ring them silver bells,
   Lord, I want to be in that number
   Oh, when they ring them silver bells.

6. And when the angels gather 'round,
   And when the angels gather 'round,
   Lord, I want to be in that number
   And when the angels gather 'round.

7. And when the Lord is shakin' hands,
   And when the Lord is shakin' hands,
   Lord, I want to be in that number
   And when the Lord is shakin' hands.

8. Oh, when the sun refuse to shine,
   Oh, when the sun refuse to shine,
   Lord, I want to be in that number
   Oh, when the sun refuse to shine.

9. Oh, when they crown Him Lord of all,
   Oh, when they crown Him Lord of all,
   Lord, I want to be in that number
   Oh, when they crown Him Lord of all.

10. Oh, when they gather 'round the throne,
    Oh, when they gather 'round the throne,
    Lord, I want to be in that number
    Oh, when they gather 'round the throne,

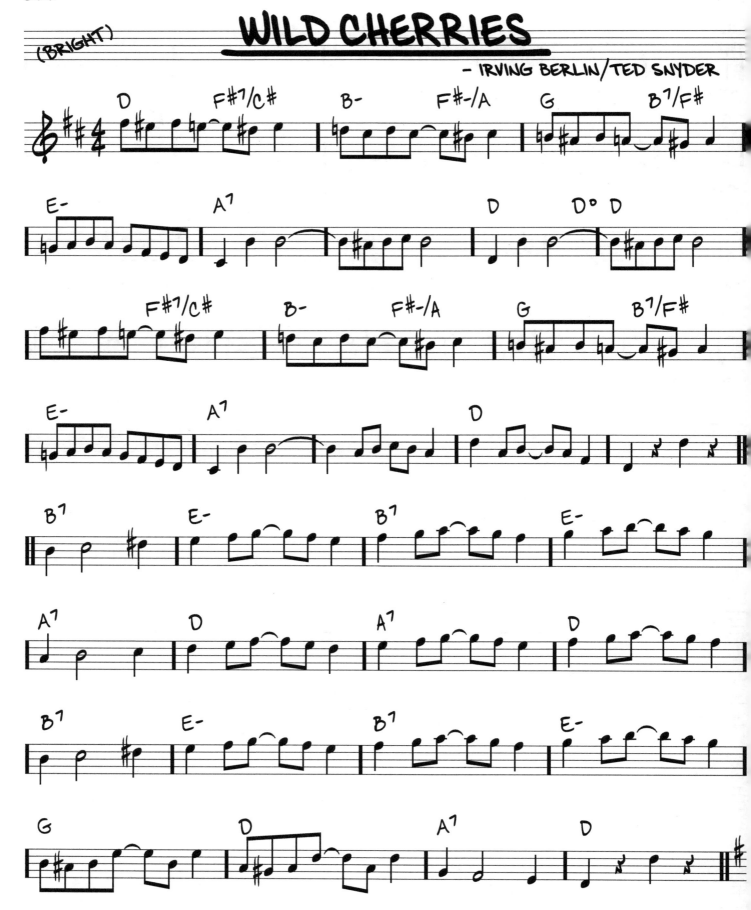

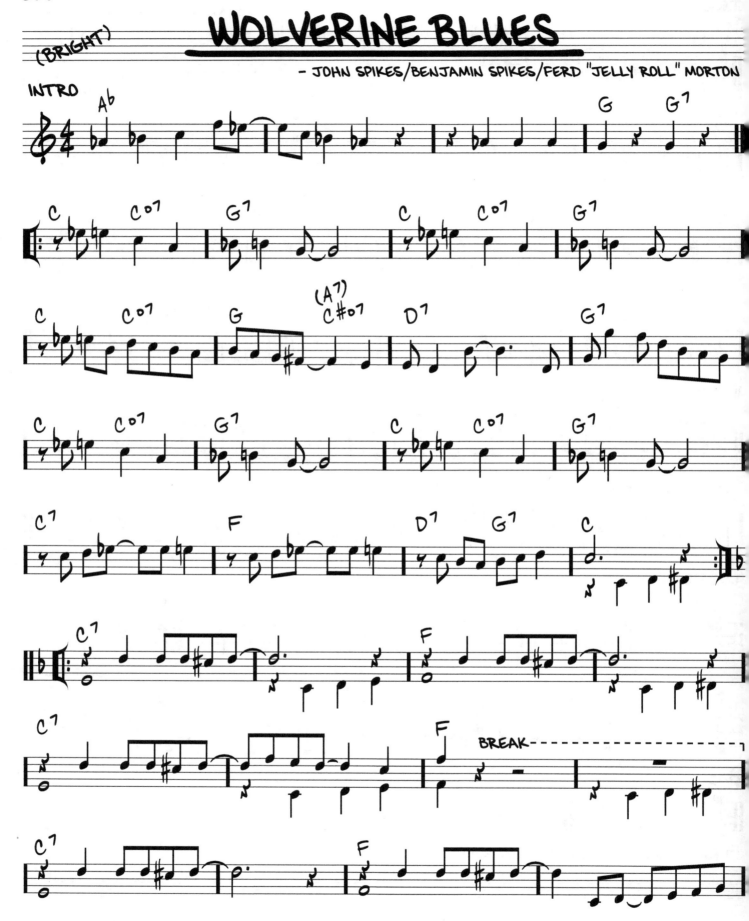

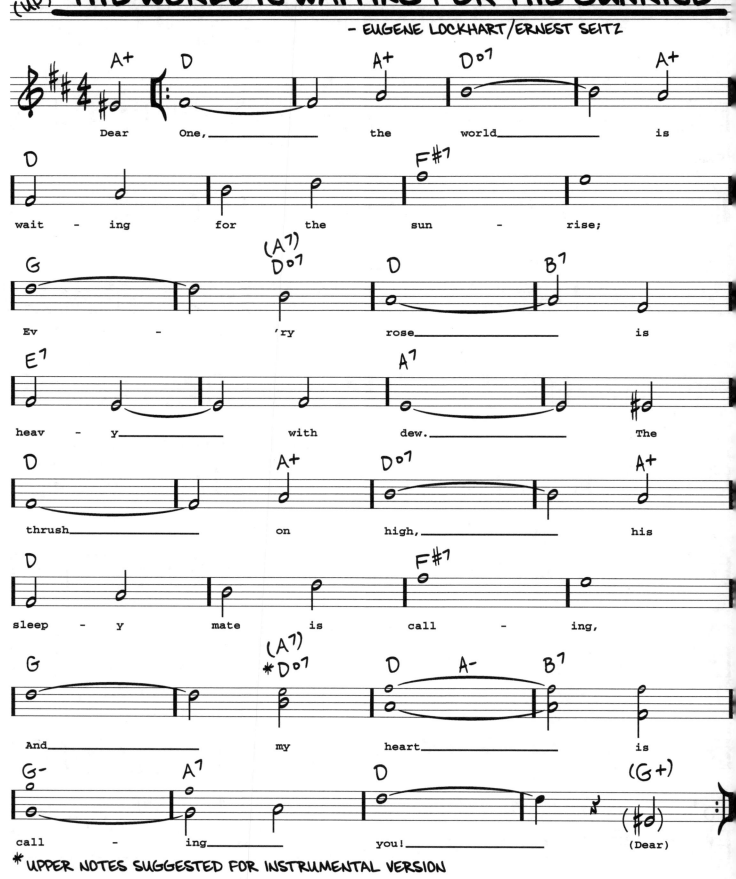

[Verse]

E'er since Miss Susan Johnson lost her Jockey, Lee,
There has been much excitement, more to be;
"Wonder where my Easy Rider's gone?"
Cablegrams come of sympathy,
Telegrams go of inquiry,
Letters come from down in "Bam",
And ev'ry where that Uncle Sam
has even a rural delivery.
All day the phone rings, but it's not for me,
At last good tidings fill our hearts with glee,
This message comes from Tennessee:

[Chorus]

Dear Sue, your Easy Rider struck his burg today
On a southboun' rattler sidedoor Pullman car.
Seen him here an' he was on the hog.
[Spoken] *The smoke was broke, no joke, not a jitney on him.*
Easy Rider got a stay way,
So he had to vamp it but the hike ain't far.
He's gone where the Southern cross' the Yellow Dog.

[Verse]

I know the Yellow Dog District like a book,
Indeed I know the route that Rider took;
Ev'ry crosstie, bayou, burg and bog.
Way down where the Southern cross' the Dog,
Money don't zactly grow on trees,
On cotton stalks it grows wid ease;
No racehorse, racetrack no grandstand
Is like Old Beck and Buckshot land,
Down where the Southern cross' the Dog.
Every kitchen there is a cabaret,
Down there the boll wevil works while the darkies glee,
This Yellow Dog Rag the livelong day.

[Chorus]

Dear Sue, your Easy Rider struck his burg today
On a southboun' rattler sidedoor Pullman car.
Seen him here an' he was on the hog.
[Spoken] *The smoke was broke, no joke, not a jitney on him.*
Easy Rider got a stay way,
So he had to vamp it but the hike ain't far.
He's gone where the Southern cross' the Yellow Dog.

The Best-Selling Jazz Book of All Time Is Now Legal!

The Real Books are the most popular jazz books of all time. Since the 1970s, musicians have trusted these volumes to get them through every gig, night after night. The problem is that the books were illegally produced and distributed, without any regard to copyright law, or royalties paid to the composers who created these musical masterpieces.

Hal Leonard is very proud to present the first legitimate and legal editions of these books ever produced. You won't even notice the difference, other than all the notorious errors being fixed: the covers and typeface look the same, the song lists are nearly identical, and the price for our edition is even cheaper than the originals!

Every conscientious musician will appreciate that these books are now produced accurately and ethically, benefitting the songwriters that we owe for some of the greatest tunes of all time!

VOLUME 1
00240221	C Edition	$35.00
00240224	B♭ Edition	$35.00
00240225	E♭ Edition	$35.00
00240226	Bass Clef Edition	$35.00
00240292	C Edition 6 x 9	$30.00
00240339	B♭ Edition 6 x 9	$30.00
00451087	C Edition on CD-ROM	$25.00
00240302	A-D CD Backing Tracks	$24.99
00240303	E-J CD Backing Tracks	$24.95
00240304	L-R CD Backing Tracks	$24.95
00240305	S-Z CD Backing Tracks	$24.99
00110604	Book/USB Flash Drive Backing Tracks Pack	$79.99
00110599	USB Flash Drive Only	$50.00

VOLUME 2
00240222	C Edition	$35.50
00240227	B♭ Edition	$35.00
00240228	E♭ Edition	$35.00
00240229	Bass Clef Edition	$35.00
00240293	C Edition 6 x 9	$30.00
00451088	C Edition on CD-ROM	$27.99
00240351	A-D CD Backing Tracks	$24.99
00240352	E-I CD Backing Tracks	$24.99
00240353	J-R CD Backing Tracks	$24.99
00240354	S-Z CD Backing Tracks	$24.99

VOLUME 3
00240233	C Edition	$35.00
00240284	B♭ Edition	$35.00
00240285	E♭ Edition	$35.00
00240286	Bass Clef Edition	$35.00
00240338	C Edition 6 x 9	$30.00
00451089	C Edition on CD-ROM	$29.99

VOLUME 4
00240296	C Edition	$35.00
00103348	B♭ Edition	$35.00
00103349	E♭ Edition	$35.00
00103350	Bass Clef Edition	$35.00

VOLUME 5
00240349	C Edition	$35.00

Also available:
00240264	The Real Blues Book	$34.99
00310910	The Real Bluegrass Book	$29.99
00240137	Miles Davis Real Book	$19.95
00240355	The Real Dixieland Book	$29.99
00240235	The Duke Ellington Real Book	$19.99
00240348	The Real Latin Book	$35.00
00240358	The Charlie Parker Real Book	$19.99
00240331	The Bud Powell Real Book	$19.99
00240313	The Real Rock Book	$35.00
00240323	The Real Rock Book – Vol. 2	$35.00
00240359	The Real Tab Book – Vol. 1	$32.50
00240317	The Real Worship Book	$29.99

THE REAL CHRISTMAS BOOK
00240306	C Edition	$29.99
00240345	B♭ Edition	$29.99
00240346	E♭ Edition	$29.99
00240347	Bass Clef Edition	$29.99
00240431	A-G CD Backing Tracks	$24.99
00240432	H-M CD Backing Tracks	$24.99
00240433	N-Y CD Backing Tracks	$24.99

THE REAL VOCAL BOOK
00240230	Volume 1 High Voice	$35.00
00240307	Volume 1 Low Voice	$35.00
00240231	Volume 2 High Voice	$35.00
00240308	Volume 2 Low Voice	$35.00
00240391	Volume 3 High Voice	$35.00
00240392	Volume 3 Low Voice	$35.00

THE REAL BOOK – STAFF PAPER
00240327		$10.99

HOW TO PLAY FROM A REAL BOOK
For All Musicians
by Robert Rawlins
00312097		$17.50

Complete song lists online at www.halleonard.com

Prices, content, and availability subject to change without notice.

7777 W. Bluemound Rd. P.O. Box 13819 Milwaukee, WI 53213

THE ULTIMATE COLLECTION OF FAKE BOOKS

The Real Book – Sixth Edition
Hal Leonard proudly presents the first legitimate and legal editions of these books ever produced. These bestselling titles are mandatory for anyone who plays jazz! Over 400 songs, including: All By Myself • Dream a Little Dream of Me • God Bless the Child • Like Someone in Love • When I Fall in Love • and more.

00240221	Volume 1, C Edition	$35.00
00240224	Volume 1, B♭ Edition	$35.00
00240225	Volume 1, E♭ Edition	$35.00
00240226	Volume 1, BC Edition	$35.00
00240222	Volume 2, C Edition	$35.00
00240227	Volume 2, B♭ Edition	$35.00
00240228	Volume 2, E♭ Edition	$35.00

Best Fake Book Ever – 4th Edition
More than 1,000 songs from all styles of music, including: All My Loving • At the Hop • Cabaret • Dust in the Wind • Fever • From a Distance • Hello, Dolly! • Hey Jude • King of the Road • Longer • Misty • Route 66 • Sentimental Journey • Somebody • Song Sung Blue • Spinning Wheel • Unchained Melody • We Will Rock You • What a Wonderful World • Wooly Bully • Y.M.C.A. • and more.
00290239 C Edition $49.99
00240083 B♭ Edition $49.95
00240084 E♭ Edition $49.95

Classic Rock Fake Book – 2nd Edition
This fake book is a great compilation of more than 250 terrific songs of the rock era, arranged for piano, voice, guitar and all C instruments. Includes: All Right Now • American Woman • Birthday • Honesty • I Shot the Sheriff • I Want You to Want Me • Imagine • It's Still Rock and Roll to Me • Lay Down Sally • Layla • My Generation • Rock and Roll All Nite • Spinning Wheel • White Room • We Will Rock You • lots more!
00240108 .... $32.50

Classical Fake Book – 2nd Edition
This unprecedented, amazingly comprehensive reference includes over 850 classical themes and melodies for all classical music lovers. Includes everything from Renaissance music to Vivaldi and Mozart to Mendelssohn. Lyrics in the original language are included when appropriate.
00240044 .... $37.50

The Disney Fake Book – 3rd Edition
Over 200 of the most beloved songs of all time, including: Be Our Guest • Can You Feel the Love Tonight • Colors of the Wind • Cruella De Vil • Friend Like Me • Heigh-Ho • It's a Small World • Mickey Mouse March • Supercalifragilisticexpialidocious • Under the Sea • When You Wish upon a Star • A Whole New World • Zip-A-Dee-Doo-Dah • and more!
00240039 .... $30.00

(Disney characters and artwork © Disney Enterprises, Inc.)

The Folksong Fake Book
Over 1,000 folksongs perfect for performers, school teachers, and hobbyists. Includes: Bury Me Not on the Lone Prairie • Clementine • Danny Boy • The Erie Canal • Go, Tell It on the Mountain • Home on the Range • Kumbaya • Michael Row the Boat Ashore • Shenandoah • Simple Gifts • Swing Low, Sweet Chariot • When Johnny Comes Marching Home • Yankee Doodle • and many more.
00240151 .... $24.95

The Hymn Fake Book
Nearly 1,000 multi-denominational hymns perfect for church musicians or hobbyists: Amazing Grace • Christ the Lord Is Risen Today • For the Beauty of the Earth • It Is Well with My Soul • A Mighty Fortress Is Our God • O for a Thousand Tongues to Sing • Praise to the Lord, the Almighty • Take My Life and Let It Be • What a Friend We Have in Jesus • and hundreds more!
00240145 .... $24.95

The Praise & Worship Fake Book
400 songs: As the Deer • Better Is One Day • Come, Now Is the Time to Worship • Firm Foundation • Glorify Thy Name • Here I Am to Worship • I Could Sing of Your Love Forever • Lord, I Lift Your Name on High • More Precious Than Silver • Open the Eyes of My Heart • The Power of Your Love • Shine, Jesus, Shine • Trading My Sorrows • We Fall Down • You Are My All in All • and more.
00240234 .... $34.95

The R&B Fake Book – 2nd Edition
This terrific fake book features 375 classic R&B hits: Baby Love • Best of My Love • Dancing in the Street • Easy • Get Ready • Heatwave • Here and Now • Just Once • Let's Get It On • The Loco-Motion • (You Make Me Feel Like) A Natural Woman • One Sweet Day • Papa Was a Rollin' Stone • Save the Best for Last • September • Sexual Healing • Shop Around • Still • Tell It Like It Is • Up on the Roof • Walk on By • What's Going On • more!
00240107 C Edition $29.95

Ultimate Broadway Fake Book – 5th Edition
More than 700 show-stoppers from over 200 shows! Includes: Ain't Misbehavin' • All I Ask of You • Bewitched • Camelot • Don't Cry for Me Argentina • Edelweiss • I Dreamed a Dream • If I Were a Rich Man • Memory • Oklahoma • Send in the Clowns • What I Did for Love • more.
00240046 .... $49.99

FOR MORE INFORMATION, SEE YOUR LOCAL MUSIC DEALER, OR WRITE TO:

7777 W. BLUEMOUND RD. P.O. BOX 13819 MILWAUKEE, WI 53213

Complete songlists available online at
www.halleonard.com

Prices, contents and availability subject to change without notice.

The Ultimate Christmas Fake Book – 5th Edition
This updated edition includes 275 traditional and contemporary Christmas songs: Away in a Manger • The Christmas Song • Deck the Hall • Frosty the Snow Man • A Holly Jolly Christmas • I Heard the Bells on Christmas Day • Jingle Bells • Little Saint Nick • Merry Christmas, Darling • Nuttin' for Christmas • Rudolph the Red-Nosed Reindeer • Silent Night • What Child Is This? • more.
00240045 .... $24.95

The Ultimate Country Fake Book – 5th Edition
This book includes over 700 of your favorite country hits: Always on My Mind • Boot Scootin' Boogie • Crazy • Down at the Twist and Shout • Forever and Ever, Amen • Friends in Low Places • The Gambler • Jambalaya • King of the Road • Sixteen Tons • There's a Tear in My Beer • Your Cheatin' Heart • and hundreds more.
00240049 .... $49.99

The Ultimate Fake Book – 5th Edition
Includes over 1,200 hits: Blue Skies • Body and Soul • Endless Love • Isn't It Romantic? • Memory • Mona Lisa • Moon River • Operator • Piano Man • Roxanne • Satin Doll • Shout • Small World • Smile • Speak Softly, Love • Strawberry Fields Forever • Tears in Heaven • Unforgettable • hundreds more!
00240024 C Edition $49.95
00240026 B♭ Edition $49.95
00240025 E♭ Edition $49.95

The Ultimate Pop/Rock Fake Book – 4th Edition
Over 600 pop standards and contemporary hits, including: All Shook Up • Another One Bites the Dust • Crying • Don't Know Much • Dust in the Wind • Earth Angel • Every Breath You Take • Hero • Hey Jude • Hold My Hand • Imagine • Layla • The Loco-Motion • Oh, Pretty Woman • On Broadway • Spinning Wheel • Stand by Me • Stayin' Alive • Tears in Heaven • True Colors • The Twist • Vision of Love • A Whole New World • Wild Thing • Wooly Bully • Yesterday • more!
00240099 .... $39.99

Fake Book of the World's Favorite Songs – 4th Edition
Over 700 favorites, including: America the Beautiful • Anchors Aweigh • Battle Hymn of the Republic • Bill Bailey, Won't You Please Come Home • Chopsticks • Für Elise • His Eye Is on the Sparrow • I Wonder Who's Kissing Her Now • Jesu, Joy of Man's Desiring • My Old Kentucky Home • Sidewalks of New York • Take Me Out to the Ball Game • When the Saints Go Marching In • and hundreds more!
00240072 .... $22.95